Charles Bradlaugh

Is it Reasonable to Worship God?

Charles Bradlaugh

Is it Reasonable to Worship God?

ISBN/EAN: 9783337852016

Printed in Europe, USA, Canada, Australia, Japan

Cover: Foto ©Lupo / pixelio.de

More available books at **www.hansebooks.com**

"IS IT REASONABLE

TO

WORSHIP GOD?"

VERBATIM REPORT

OF

TWO NIGHTS' DEBATE AT NOTTINGHAM

BETWEEN

THE REV. R. A. ARMSTRONG

AND

CHARLES BRADLAUGH.

LONDON:
FREETHOUGHT PUBLISHING COMPANY,
28, STONECUTTER STREET, E.C.

1878.

LONDON :
PRINTED BY ANNIE BESANT AND CHARLES BRADLAUGH,
28, STONECUTTER STREET.

PREFACE.

I HAVE been invited to prefix a few sentences to this debate in its published form, and I am glad to avail myself of the opportunity so courteously accorded.

Many have criticised my conduct in consenting to meet in public debate one whose teachings, both theological (or anti-theological) and social, they and I alike regard as in many respects of pernicious tendency. My reply is, that those teachings are influencing large numbers of men and women; that to denounce them, is simply to intensify their influence in some quarters; and that they must be met face to face if their force is to be diminished. I regard oral public discussion as one of the least efficient methods for the discovery of truth; but I cannot blind myself to the fact that it is almost the only method by which what I hold to be true, can get the ear and the attention of some classes of the community; and I perceive that if a man can trust his temper and is also interested in his cause and not in himself, he may in this way do some good which he can do in no other. If it be given him to touch one heart or enlighten one soul, it is a cheap price to pay, that a laugh may go against him, or even that some good and sincere persons may think he has acted wrongly.

The debate itself can only touch the edge of subjects so stupendous as Theism and Worship. But some may be led by it to thought or to study, on which they would not otherwise have entered.

I select three points in this debate for a further word or two:

(1.) I said Mr. Bradlaugh could not "conceive a better world." The expression is ambiguous. He and I both conceive and strive to promote a better state of things than that now existing. But we can conceive no better constitution for a world than that of a world so constituted as to evoke the effort of mankind to advance its progress and improvement. The evil is not in itself good; it is only the necessary condition of good. The moment you conceive a world existing from first to last without evil, you conceive a world destitute of the necessary conditions for the evolution of noble character; and so, in eliminating the evil, you eliminate a good which a thousand times outweighs the evil.

(2.) "Either," argues Mr. Bradlaugh, in effect, "God could make a world without suffering, or he could not. If he could and did not, he is not all-good. It he could not, he is not all-powerful." The reply is, What do you mean by all-powerful? If you mean having power to reconcile things in themselves contradictory, we do not hold that God is all-powerful. But a humanity, from the first enjoying immunity from suffering, and yet possessed of nobility of character, is a self-contradictory conception.

(3.) I have ventured upon alleging an Intelligent Cause of the phenomena of the universe; in spite of the fact that in several of his writings Mr. Bradlaugh has described intelligence as implying limitations. But though intelligence, as known to us in man, is always hedged within limits, there is no difficulty in conceiving each and every limit as removed. In that case the essential conception of intelligence remains the same precisely, although the change of conditions revolutionises its mode of working.

The metaphysical argument for Theism, though I hold it in the last resort to be unanswerable, can never be the real basis of personal religion. That must rest on the facts of consciousness verified by the results in character flowing from the candid recognition of those facts. It is useless, as well as unscientific, for the Atheist either to deny or to ignore those facts. The hopeless task that lies before him, ere Theism can be overturned, is to prove that experiences which to many a Theist are more real and more unquestionable than the deliverances of sight, of hearing, or of touch, are mere phantasies of the brain.

I addressed the following letter to the Editor of the *National Reformer* after the debate.

TO THE EDITOR OF THE "NATIONAL REFORMER."

SIR,—Some of those who heard or may read the recent discussion between Mr. Bradlaugh and myself may be willing to pursue the positive argument for Theism and Worship which I adopted—as distinguished from and supplementary to the ordinary metaphysical argument—at greater length than the limits of time permitted me to expound it in the debate. Will you allow me to recommend to such persons three works which will specially serve their purpose? These are—Theodore Parker's "Discourse of Matters Pertaining to Religion" (eighteenpence, British and Foreign Unitarian Association, 37, Norfolk Street, Strand); F. W. Newman's "Hebrew Theism" (half-a-crown, Trübner); and the Rev. Charles Voysey's "Mystery of Pain, Death, and Sin" (Williams & Norgate, 1878). I would gladly add to these Professor Blackie's "Natural History of Atheism"—a book of much intellectual force—were it not that he indulges too often in a strain of superior contempt with which I have no sympathy.—I am, &c.,

RICHARD A. ARMSTRONG.

NOTTINGHAM,
    Sept. 9th, 1878.

I only now further desire to refer the reader to Mr. Brownlow Maitland's "Theism or Agnosticism" (eighteen-pence, Christian Knowledge Society, 1878).

Tennyson shall utter for me my last plea with the doubter to throw himself upon the bosom of God in prayer :—

> "Speak to him, thou, for he hears, and spirit with spirit can meet,—
> Closer is he than breathing, and nearer than hands and feet."

R. A. ARMSTRONG.

NOTTINGHAM,
Sept. 23rd, 1878.

"IS IT REASONABLE TO WORSHIP GOD?"

The first of two nights' debate in the Co-operative Hall, Nottingham, between the Rev. R. A. Armstrong and Mr. Charles Bradlaugh; G. B. Rothera, Esq., in the chair.

The CHAIRMAN: Ladies and Gentlemen,—I have had the pleasure, during the last few weeks, of spending a very pleasant holiday on the heather-covered mountains of Scotland. On reaching Edinburgh on my way homeward, I received a letter from my friend, Mr. Armstrong, informing me of the arrangements for to-night's debate, and of the wish that was felt that I should preside. Though a private communication, yet as it contains the grounds upon which the request was made, and in part also those upon which I was induced to comply, I shall be glad if Mr. Armstrong will kindly give me permission to read that letter to you. It is as follows:—

"MY DEAR SIR,—I have obtained your address from your son, and you must blame him for enabling me to molest you with my importunities in the midst of your holiday.

"Circumstances have led to my receiving an invitation from the local branch of the National Secular Society, and from Mr. Bradlaugh, to debate with the latter on the reasonableness of religious worship. At first strongly disposed to decline, I have been led, together with the friends whom I have consulted, to believe that it was my duty to accept the task, and, however distasteful, I am now in for it.

"It is to take place at the Co-operative Hall, on two consecutive nights, Thursday and Friday, September 5 and 6, and we are most anxious to secure the services—which I hope will be chiefly formal—of a competent chairman who will possess the respect of both parties. My own friends and the Secularists independently suggested your name, and we all feel that we should be deeply indebted to you if you would preside over us on the two nights. My earnest desire is to throw such a tone into the meetings as shall make them really helpful to genuine truth-seekers, and I have good ground for believing that many such will be present.

"I sincerely hope you will do us all this favour. I do not know where else to turn for a chairman that will be so acceptable to all concerned. Your speedy and favourable reply will be very welcome to yours truly, R. A. ARMSTRONG.

"Burns Street, Nottingham, Aug. 24, 1878.

"G. B. ROTHERA, Esq."

Now, ladies and gentlemen, on receiving that letter my first impulse was, I think naturally, to decline, and that for two reasons—first, I find that as one gets on in life there is a stronger and stronger disposition to avoid the excitement of public meetings, to seek more and more the ease of one's own arm-chair, and to enjoy that best of all society, our books (hear). Beyond this I had real misgivings as to my ability to fill, as I ought, the duties sought to be put upon me. Nevertheless, on slight reflection, these difficulties vanished. I felt that there were occasions, of which this, probably, was one, when it becomes us to lay aside considerations of personal ease and convenience in the hope to meet the wishes of, and to be useful to, one's neighbours and friends. Now, in occupying this position I must not be considered to identify myself with either the one party or the other (hear). I may agree with either, or with neither. I am here, as I believe you are here, interested in a question of the gravest concern to all of us, as an earnest inquirer, anxious to learn and not afraid to hear (applause). My position, I take it, is very much akin to that of the Speaker of the House of Commons. I have simply to regulate the order of debate, and to ask at your hands —what I am sure I shall receive—such orderly and consistent behaviour as will become an assembly of English gentlemen. Now, in those who have charged themselves with the responsibility of this debate we have men of acknowledged ability and high culture (applause)—men who, I am sure will know well how to reconcile the duties of courtesy with the earnestness of debate. In addressing themselves to the present question, it must, I think, be clearly understood that the question, as it appears upon the paper, is not to be narrowed to a simple inquiry whether it is reasonable that we should worship God. A much wider issue must be covered by the debate, if it is to satisfy the expectations of this audience. The question is one, I take, it between

Theism and Atheism. It is not enough to postulate a Deity, and then ask whether it is reasonable or not to worship him. What I think we have a right to ask is, that the gentleman charged with the affirmative of the proposition shall adduce such evidence as will establish satisfactorily the conclusion that there is a Deity to worship. The position of the Atheist, I take it, is not one of disbelief, but of simple unbelief. He does not say that God is not, but he affirms the lack of evidence for the position that God is (hear). He does not even say that there may not be a God. What he does say is that if there is a God he has failed to manifest himself, either by the utterance of his voice, in audible revelation, or by the impression of his hand upon visible nature. I take it, therefore, and think Mr. Armstrong will be prepared to accept the position, that it will be incumbent upon him, at the outset of the discussion, to address himself to a consideration of the proofs in favour of the position that there is a God to worship. If he succeed in this, then, I think, there will be a very difficult and trying ordeal before Mr. Bradlaugh to prove that, God, being existent, is not entitled to the reasonable worship of his creatures (applause). Pardon me these remarks by way of introduction. Before calling on Mr. Armstrong to open the debate, I may just say that, by arrangement between them, Mr. Armstrong, upon whom the affirmative rests, is to be allowed half-an-hour to open the discussion; Mr. Bradlaugh half-an-hour in reply; that then the next hour will be divided into quarters, each speaker having a quarter of an hour alternately (applause). The result of this arrangement will be that Mr. Armstrong will open the debate to-night, which will be closed by Mr. Bradlaugh, while to-morrow night Mr. Bradlaugh will open the debate and Mr. Armstrong will close it. This, I think, you will regard as a satisfactory arrangement, and a liberal one, inasmuch as Mr. Bradlaugh concedes to Mr. Armstrong the advantage of the last word (applause).

Mr. ARMSTRONG, who was cordially received, said: Mr. Chairman and friends—I wish to say two or three words at the outset of this debate as to its origin. You are many of you aware that a short time ago Mr. Bradlaugh visited this town, and gave a lecture in defence of Atheism, from this platform, in answer to Professor Max Müller's Hibbert lectures. I was led to be present then, and I offered some remarks at the close. Mr. Bradlaugh rejoined, and in the course of his rejoinder threw out, in a courteous manner, a challenge for me to meet him and discuss these weighty matters at further length. I thought no more of it then, not conceiving it to be my duty to take up that challenge. A few days afterwards, however, I received a letter from the Secretary of the Nottingham branch of the National Secular Society stating that many persons had been much interested in the words that fell from me, and that they would consider it an obligation conferred upon them, and others earnestly in pursuit of truth, if I consented to meet Mr. Bradlaugh in this manner. I replied, that for my own part, I was but little sanguine of any good effects, or a balance of good effects, resulting from such a meeting; but that the invitation being couched in such courteous and earnest terms, I would consult with friends on whose judgment I placed reliance, before finally replying. I consulted these friends, and at the same time thought the matter over further; and I came to the conclusion that, though it has undoubtedly happened that on too many occasions theological debates have been the root of bitterness and strife, yet, nevertheless, two men really in earnest about what they have to say, and speaking to persons also in earnest, who have come neither for amusement nor excitement—I came to the conclusion that a debate, conducted with tact and temper on both sides, might (may I say by the blessing of God?) conduce rather to good than to evil (applause). Under these circumstances, I accepted the challenge. I did so, though, as I said in my letter to the chairman, it is distasteful to me, because if I make anything of this occasion it can only be by exhibiting to you my inmost heart. We are not going to talk in a superficial manner—we are not going to bandy compliments, nor, I hope, exchange rebukes; but, each of us is going to search his inner consciousness, and try to express to the audience that which he finds therein. It is, perhaps, more distasteful to me on this occasion than to Mr. Bradlaugh, since I find, or believe myself to find, in my inner consciousness certain facts which Mr. Bradlaugh will no doubt tell you he does not find in his inner consciousness. These facts are to me of the most solemn and sacred nature conceivable, and to expose them before a large and public audience is a thing very like a sort of martyrdom. If I were not confident that, however little you may sympathise with what I say, you will treat it with respect or consideration, I woul' never consent to drag the sacred thoughts of my soul before you to hold them up as an exhibition (hear). I am to maintain to-night—not to demonstrate (as you will see if you look at the bills)—the proposition that it is reasonable to worship God. Mr. Bradlaugh has not necessarily to disprove, but to impugn, that proposition. Now, all I have any hope of doing to-night is this—to show that it is reasonable for me and for others conscious of mental phenomena in themselves more or less akin to those of which I am conscious, to worship God. Would that I could touch you with the beauty and the sweetness of this belief—would that I could hold up before you, in all its glory and sublimity, in all its strength and holiness, the beauty and the sweetness of the worship of God. Could I succeed in doing so, I should take your imaginations captive. I think I should get the suffrage of your reason. It is as though, sir, to-night, I had been called upon to prove that my dearest friend is worthy to be loved—ay, even that my dearest friend exists; for, if God is aught to us, he is our dearest, nearest friend—present when all others are taken from us, a sure refuge in every moment of temptation and of woe; the very highest and most intimate reality of which the mind can conceive—the sum and substance of all existence. Well, now, how do I know this God? Who is this God of whom I speak? Let me try to tell you how it seems to me that I have made acquaintance with him. I find that at certain moments of my life there is that which I can best describe as a voice—though it is a metaphor—addressed to me, influencing largely my conduct. I find that there are in me, as in all men, strong instincts, strong desires, strong self-interests—some lower, some higher, some less worthy, some more worthy, than others. I find that but for this voice of which I speak I should be entirely swayed thereby, as, so far as I can see, the brutes of the field and the forest are swayed thereby. But I find that sometimes, at moments when these instincts are the very strongest within me, and when I am about to throw myself into their realisation and give them expression in fact—I find, sometimes, at these moments that there comes to me somewhat which, so far as my consciousness delivers, is not myself. There comes to me somewhat stopping me from indulging these instincts and bidding me to curb them. I find at other times that my instincts of self-preservation, of self-regard, of pleasure-loving, and so forth—my appetites—

would lead me to hold back from a certain course of action. So far as I can judge, looking into my own mind, myself is against that course of action. It appears to my reasoning powers and inclinations that I had better keep out of it. But there comes now somewhat which comes from outside, and which is no part of myself, which says, "Go and do it." That was so when I received the invitation to this debate. Again, I find that on certain occasions—alas! that I should have to say it—I have defied this monitor, I have done that which it told me not to do, or not done that which it bade me to do. I find then that there enter into me from somewhere—I know not from whence—pangs of remorse keener than ever came from any personal sorrow, more biting than ever came from any physical pain. There have been times, however—let me thank God I can say so!—when I have obeyed this voice, followed its dictates in spite of all myself seeming to drag me from it; and my experience is that on these occasions there has entered my soul, from whence I cannot tell you, a peace surpassing that given us in any other circumstances—a peace in the light of which the sorrows that at other times might cut me to the heart seem light and small, a peace in the beauty and holiness of which these sorrows seem wonderfully diminished. I will tell you what I call the source of that voice which I fancy speaks to me in that fourfold manner. I call the source of that voice "God," and that is the first thing I mean by God. I call the source of all these monitions and admonitions, these exhortations and rebukes, this voice of reproval and of approval, the voice of God; because I must give it some name, and that seems to me the simplest and the truest name I can give it. I might, perhaps, be inclined to doubt whether all this was not fancy (though I hardly think I should) if, so far as I could gather, it were an unique experience of my own; but I find that it is not so. I find that this voice is recognised by every true man and woman I meet. They may obey it or not, but they recognise it, and allow that it is there. I behold the picture by Millais of the day before the awful massacre of St. Bartholomew. I see the maiden leaning on her lover's bosom whilst he looks down upon her with looks of love and tenderness, and she strives to tie around his arm a scarf. She knows of the impending massacre, that all Protestants are to be slaughtered, and she would fain put this badge upon his arm as a secret signal to preserve him from the sword. Does he accept this method of escape? Although his inclination is to remain with his beloved, the strength of his right hand is given to tear the badge from his arm, and he faces death, not with joy, but with an exceeding bitter sorrow for the moment—he faces death in simple loyalty and obedience to the voice which has spoken to his heart. That is an experience which you will all recognise—one which, in less or in greater force, we have all had. Whatever explanation may be given—and, doubtless, Mr. Brad! laugh has an explanation of his own—this voice of conscience is to me one of the primary evidences of the existence of God. Nay, I will not call it an evidence; it is God speaking to me (applause). This conscience has been described by Mr. Voysey, in his recently-published sermons in refutation of Atheism, as follows: "The collision is so complete between the higher voice and the impelling instinct, that one can only feel that the two are radically different in nature, and must have had a different source. . . . To have the power of doing intentionally what one shrinks from doing, and to deny one's self the pleasure which is so fascinating, and which one longs to do, is to prove the immense superiority of our inner selves over the visible universe." To have the power, as that man, that Huguenot, must have had it, to deny one's self the pleasure which is so fascinating, and for which one longs, is to prove the immense superiority of our inner selves when hearing the voice of God over the visible universe. Again, speaking of conscience, Voysey says: "The conscience which makes us mortify our flesh with its affections and lusts, and which often mars our happiness and embitters our pleasure, upbraids us with reproaches and stings us with remorse, that voice which hushes our cry for happiness, which will not endure a single selfish plea, but demands unquestioning obedience, and bids us fall down in the very dust before the Majesty of Duty—we all, in our secret hearts, revere this power, whether or not we obey it as we should. At least, we pay to it the homage of our inmost souls, and feel how great and grand it is to be its slave." Now, sir, I desire to pass on to another method, by which it seems to me that I apprehend this being. Having made the acquaintance with this awful voice—and the philosopher Kant said two things filled him with awe, the starry heavens and the moral nature in man—I pass on to another matter. Behold the starry heaven itself. I know not how it is with you, but I will tell you my experience—and we are told by scientific men that we must bring everything to the test of experience. Sometimes when I have been out of temper—as I am sometimes, like other people—sometimes, when I have been much distracted with cares, when troubles and pains have been thick upon me, it falls to my lot to go out beneath the starry heaven. What is it that I experience in my soul? I go through no process of metaphysical reasoning, I do not argue with myself, but I simply feel that there is a Divine presence there, in whose hand are all these stars and all these worlds—a great voice singing, "I am strong and I am good, and you are safe nestling in my hand." I know not if that corresponds with the experience of all here, but that it corresponds with the experience of many, I feel sure; and let me ask such not to drive away these holy feelings, but to trust them as the assurance which God gives of his presence. It may be that in those lakes and mountains which you, sir, have seen of late, you may have heard a message whispering to your soul of a peace beyond the peace of earth—of a presence before which all things are well. In others, not so sensitive perhaps to the beauties of natural scenery, such experience comes in the tones of music—in some grand symphony or some sweet song; and they feel lifted away from the things of earth, and they feel lifted into some presence in which it is a joy to be, and which fills their soul with peace. That presence I call, having no other name for it, the presence of God. Observe, that in this I am not philosophising about the cause—I am not saying that God is the cause and so on; I am only relating the experience of my consciousness, reported to you as faithfully and truly as I can read it. Let me read what Professor Blackie wrote the other day: "Many things can be known only by being felt, all vital forces are fundamentally unknowable." And, says Francis Newman, that arch-heretic: "The astronomer is ever aware of the presence of gravitation and the electrician sees all things pervaded by electricity—powers descried by the mind, unwitnessed by any sense, long unknown to the wise, still unknown or undiscerned by the vulgar; yet this perception of things hidden is not esteemed cloudy." Now, having made some acquaintance with this awful, inscrutable something, to which I venture to give the name of God, I venture to lift up to it the voice of my soul, and strive to throw myself towards that Being. And what is my experience? Let us go to experience again: I find when my mind is bewildered and in doubt, when it is all involved with difficulties, that somehow, when I address that Being, there comes to my soul "clear-shining," and I see things plainer and more beautiful than before. I appeal to him in pain and sorrow—not with the coward's prayer, but simply asking that I may feel his presence, to endure it; and the pain and sorrow have become light on the instant assurance that God is there to comfort and console. I pray to him in weakness, when my strength fails, and what is the result? That a new manhood comes to me, and I feel that wondrous power which over-arches all the worlds, and I feel that I have in me also somewhat of his strength. I appeal to him, last of all, in temptation, when the wrong deed presses closely on my inclinations, and what do I find? That strength is given me to stand up against temptation, and he answers according to the immemorial prayer of Christendom: deliver us from temptation. This is experience, or I fancy it is. It is not theory. Again, I am in gladness. When is my gladness greatest, and when is it richest? Why, when it flows up and out, in thankfulness and adoration, to the source to which I trace it. Then my gladness seems to receive an influence which lifts it up above. No gladness is the true gladness without that. Let me conclude this half-hour by reading a very short extract from Professor Newman. Speaking of the instincts of mankind, he says:—

And the instinct of Religion is the noblest of them all,
The bravest, the most enduring, the most fruitful in mighty deeds,
The source of earliest grandeur, unitress of scattered tribes;
Even in the crudeness of its infancy,when unpurified by science,
Yet teeming with civilisation, with statesmanship, with letters.
Mistress of all high art, and parent of glorious martyrs.
And if from it have come wars, and bigotries, and cruelties,
Through infantine hot-headedness and unripeness of mind,
We take your aid, O Sceptics! to purge it from all such evils,
And kindly honour we pay to you for your battles against superstition;
Yet the very evils ye deplore, prove Religion's mighty energy,
And the grasp deeply seated which she has within human hearts."

(Loud applause.)

Mr. Bradlaugh: Thanking you, sir, for acceding to the request which I would have gladly joined in had I had any right of acquaintance to entitle me to make it; thanking you for undertaking what is always a troublesome duty, however well a debate may be conducted, of presiding over a discussion, permit me to say one word only as to the opening which fell from your lips. There is only one phrase in that which I desire to note, so as to save myself from the possibility of misapprehension. I quite agree with the view you put of the position the Atheist takes, except that if Dualism be affirmed, if more than Monism be affirmed, if more than one existence be affirmed, and if it be the beyond of that one existence which is called God, then the Atheist does not say there may be one, but says there cannot be one; and that is the only distinction I wish to put as against the very kind words with which you introduced the speakers this evening The question for our debate is : "Is it reasonable to worship God?" and to determine this question it is necessary to define the words "worship" and "God," and next to decide whether belief in God is reasonable or unreasonable; and, secondly, whether worship is, under any, and if any, what, circumstances, reasonable or unreasonable. And I am afraid I must here except that, in the speech to which I have just listened, and which, from its tone and kindly style, is perfectly unexceptionable, there is not one word at present—it may possibly come later on—which may fairly be taken as approaching a definition either of the word "God" or the word "worship." By worship I mean act of reverence, respect, adoration, homage, offered to some person. According to this definition, worship cannot be offered to the impersonal, and according to this definition it would be unreasonable to advocate worship to be offered to the impersonal. Under the term "worship" I include prayer—which is, evidently, from the opening, also included in the term "worship" by the rev. gentleman who maintains the opposite position to myself—praise, sacrifice, offerings, solemn services, adoration, personal prostration. For the word "God," not having a definition of my own, I take—not having yet gathered, in what has fallen from Mr. Armstrong, enough to enable me to say that I understand what he means by it—I take the definition of "God" given in Professor Flint's Baird lectures; not meaning by that that Mr. Armstrong is bound by that definition, but asking him to be kind enough to note where he thinks that definition is incorrect, and to kindly tell me so, for my guidance in the latter portions of the debate. By "God," for the purpose of this debate, I shall mean a self-existent, eternal being, infinite in power and in wisdom, and perfect in holiness and goodness ; the maker of heaven and earth. And by "self-existent" I mean, that, the conception of which does not require the conception of antecedent to it. For example, this glass is phenomenal, conceived, as all phenomena must be conceived, by the characteristics or qualities which enable you to think and identify it in your mind, but which cannot be conceived except as that of which there is possible antecedent and consequent, and which, therefore, cannot be considered as self-existent according to my definition. By "eternal" and by "infinite" I only mean illimitable, indefinite, to me—applying the term "eternal" to duration, and the word "infinite" to extension. I take Professor Flint, or whoever may hold the definition I have given of God, by "maker" to mean originator; and then I am in the difficulty that the word "creator," in the sense of origin, is, to me, a word without meaning. I only know creation as change ; origin of phenomena, not of existence; origin of condition, not origin of substance. The words "creation" and "destruction" are both words which have no other meaning to my mind than the meaning of change. I will now try to address myself to some of the arguments that were put forward by Mr. Armstrong. He said that to him the notion of entering into this debate was distasteful to him, and he addressed somewhat of an inquiry as to my own feeling on the matter. No! the discussion of no one subject more than any other is distasteful to me, unless it be of a personal character, in which it might involve my having to say things upon which I should not like to mislead and upon which it would be painful to me to state the facts. Then a discussion would be distasteful to me ; but such a discussion as this is not any more distasteful to me than the discussion of an astronomical or geological problem ; and I will urge to those who go even further and say, that not only is such a matter distasteful, but that the discussion of Theism is really immoral, to such I would read from a recent volume entitled "A Candid Examination of Theism":—"If there is no God, where can be the harm in our examining the spurious evidence of his existence? If there is a God, surely our first duty towards him must be to exert to our utmost, in our attempts to find him, the most noble faculty with which he has endowed us—as carefully to investigate the evidence which he has seen fit to furnish of his own existence, as we investigate the evidence of inferior things in his dependent creation. To say that there is one rule or method for ascertaining truth in the latter case which it is not legitimate to apply in the former case, is merely a covert way of saying that the Deity—if he exists—has not supplied us with rational evidence of his existence." Now, that is the position I am going to put to you; and there ought to be nothing distasteful to anyone in proving most thoroughly the whole of the evidence upon which his supposed belief in God's existence rests. The grounds of his belief ought to be clear to himself, or they are no sufficient grounds for his belief, even to himself. If they are clear to himself they ought to be clearly stateable to others; because, if not, they lie under the suspicion of not being clear to himself. That which is sufficient to him to convince him, is either capable of being clearly stated—although it may not carry conviction to another—or it is not. If it is not capable of being clearly stated, I would suggest it is because it does not clearly exist in his own mind. Now Mr. Armstrong says that he feels as if called upon to prove that his dearest friend ought to be loved, as if called upon to prove that his dearest friend exists. He spoke of God as being to him his dearest friend, and he followed that with some words as to which I am not quite sure whether he intended to use them in the sense in which they fell upon my ears. He described God as "the sum and substance of all existence." I do not want to make any verbal trick, and if I am putting more on Mr. Armstrong than he meant to convey I should like to be put right when he rises again, and I will ask him if he considers God to be the sum and substance of all existing; and, if he does not, I will ask him in what respect he distinguishes between God, in his mind, and the sum and substance of all existence; because clearly, when he used those words he had some meaning in his mind, and I should like to know these two things: First, do you identify God in your mind with the sum and substance of all existence? If not, in what respects do you distinguish God in your mind from the sum and substance of all existence? If you say that you identify God with the sum and substance of all existence, then I ask, are we included in that sum and substance of all existence? And if we are included in that sum and substance of all existence, is it reasonable for one phenomenon or for a number of phenomena, to offer worship to any of, and to how much of, what remains? Then he addressed himself to the very old argument, which he put so beautifully, when he said: "How do I know God?" and launched into what is known as the argument from conscience, an argument very fully stated by Professor Flint in the Baird lectures to which I have referred. Mr. Armstrong said, and here I will take a little exception; he said: "In me, as in all men here, are strong instincts; in me, as in all men, there are strong desires; in me, as in all men, there is a voice." That is just the blunder; that is not true. I do not mean that in any sort of disrespectful sense. If you take a volume like Topinard's "Anthropology" you find that men's desires, men's emotions, and men's instincts all vary with race, all vary with locality, with type, all vary with what Buckle called "Food, climate, soil, and life surroundings;" and I ask, if there be this variance in individuals of different races, nay, more, if there be this variance in individuals of the same race at the same moment, and if the members of the same race vary in different places and ages, as to their instincts, desires, and emotions, I ask you whether there has been the same variation in the source of it? You say the source is God, and if so, how can a variable source be a reliable object of worship? Then let us see a little more. "I do not desire to do something, but my monitor says 'Do;'" or the reverse; and thus voice is the evidence of Deity. I should have been obliged if Mr. Armstrong had defined exactly what it was he meant by conscience, because here we are going terribly to disagree. I am going to deny the existence of conscience altogether, except as a result of development upon organisation, including in that, transmitted predisposition of ability to possible thought or action. But if that be so, what becomes of this "still small voice," of those desires and instincts? The mere fact that the mother may have worked in a cotton-mill while childbearing and have had bad food, or that the father may have beaten her—his brutality may result in the awakening of a desire and instinct exactly the opposite of that which Mr. Armstrong has, and the organisation fitted for repeating which may be handed down through generations. I stood this morning for other purposes at the doors of Coldbathfields Prison. One man who came out gave a sort of shrill whistle and plunged into the crowd with a defiant and a mocking air, showing that his conscience, his monitor, said nothing to him except that he was glad he was outside, and ready to war with the world again (applause). I am not wishing to press this view in any fashion unkindly or unfairly; I am only wanting to put the thing as it appears to me. I want to know: "Does Mr. Armstrong contend that there is a faculty identical in every human being which he calls conscience, which does decide for each human being, and always decides, in the same manner, what is right and what is wrong? Or does he mean that this 'monitor,' as he calls it, decides differently in different men and in different countries? And if 'yes,' is the source different in each case where there is a different expression? And if 'yes,' is it justifiable and reasonable to offer worship to an uncertain source, or to a source which speaks with a different voice, or to a source which is only one of a number, and of which you do not know how far its limit extends, and where its jurisdiction begins or ends?" Let us follow this out a little more. We have not only to define conscience, but we have also to define right and wrong, and I did not hear Mr. Armstrong do that. I did hear him say that when he had done something in opposition to his monitor he felt remorse. I did hear him say there was struggling between himself and his monitor, and here I had another difficulty. What is the himself that struggles, as distinguished in his mind from the monitor that he struggles against? If the struggle is a mental one, what is mind struggling against? and if it is not, how does Mr. Armstrong explain it? Let us, if you please, go to right and wrong. By moral I mean useful. I mean that that is right which tends to the greatest happiness of the greatest number, with the least injury to any. I am only following Jeremy Bentham. That is my definition of right. Many matters which have been held to come within that definition in one age have been found in another age not to come within it, and the great march of civilisation is that from day to day it instructs us in what is useful. I submit that instead of adoring the source of contradictory verdicts it is more reasonable to find out for ourselves some rule we can apply. For example, here Mr. Armstrong's conscience would not raise any particular objection to his taking animal food, unless he happens to be a vegetarian, and then, I am sure, he would conscientiously carry it out; but the majority of people's consciences in England would raise no great objection to taking animal food. Yet in China and in Hindustan hundreds of thousands of human beings have died because vegetable food was not there for them, and their consciences made them prefer death to tasting animal food. I want to know whether the conscience is from the same source here as in Hindustan, and I want to know, if that is so, which people are justified in worshipping the source? Take the case of murder. Mr. Armstrong's conscience would clearly tell him that it was wrong to murder me. And yet there are many people in this country who would not go to that extent. But I am going to take a stronger illustration. There are a number of people who think it perfectly right to bless the flags of a regiment, and to pray to the God whom Mr. Armstrong asks me to worship, that a particular regiment, whose flags are blessed, may kill the people of some other particular regiment as rapidly as possible. This shows that there are confusions of mind as to what is meant by murder, and a like confusion exists on a number of other matters on which the monitor is misrepresenting. And then Mr. Armstrong has said, "I mean by God the source of admonition, rebukes, remorse, trouble," and he says: "It is a conscience-voice which is recognised by every true man and woman." I am sure he would not wish to put any position stronger than it should be put, and he put it, too, that this was the feature in which man differed from the brutes. I am inclined to tell him that not only there is not that recognition to-day amongst the physiological and psychological teachers, but that we have a number of men whose researches have been collected for us, who show us that what you call the "still small voice," this monitor, these desires, instincts, emotions, are to be found—varied, it is true —right through the whole scale of animal life. Wherever there is a nervous encephalic apparatus sufficient you have—except in the fact of language—wider distinction between the highest order of human race and the lowest, than you have between the lowest order of human beings and those whom you are pleased to call brutes. I will now only take the illustration of the eve of St. Bartholomew, which is fatal to the argument of Mr. Armstrong. He gave the Protestant lover—a very fine character—rejecting the symbolic bandage, and preferring to die for his faith; or, as Mr. Armstrong put it, "to face death in simple loyalty rather than play the hypocrite, and the source of that feeling was God." Was that the source of the feeling which led Bruno to be burnt at the stake as if for Atheism, or for Vanini, burnt for Atheism; or for Lescynski, burnt for Atheism; or for Mrs. Besant, robbed of her child because of her avowal of Atheism (hisses)? You are hissing; wait whilst I answer. Is the source of your hissing, God? Then what a cowardly and weak thing, and little fitted for worship must be that source (applause). I desire to deal with this subject in all gravity, in all sincerity, in all kindness, but I plead for a cause—weakly, it is true—for which great and brave men and women have died, and I will permit no insult to it in my presence—(cheers)—knowingly I will pass none. I believe my antagonist to meet me loyally, honourably, and honestly, and I believe him to meet me earnestly and sincerely. I believe he has no desire to wound my feelings, and I do not wish to wound his; and I ask you, the jury here, to try to follow the same example set by him in this debate (cheers).

Mr. ARMSTRONG, being received with cheers, said: It is very difficult indeed to think on these deep problems under consideration with excitement amongst the audience present, therefore I hope that you will be as quiet as you can. I will begin at once with a confession —and this, at any rate, will be a testimony of my candour— by saying that the moment I had spoken certain words in my opening speech I thought: "Mr. Bradlaugh will have me there;" and he had me (laughter). The words were those in which I spoke of God as the sum and substance of all existence. Now, to me, God is a much simpler word than the phrase, "sum and substance of all existence." Whether God be the "sum and substance of all existence" I know not, for those words convey to me less clear meaning than the word "God" conveys to me. The source, moreover, of my immediate knowledge of God is such that it can make no asseverations whatever upon deep questions of metaphysics, as to what the "sum and substance of all existence" may consist. Mr. Bradlaugh has taken a definition of God from Professor Flint. He is a Scotchman, and Scotchmen are very fond of definitions (a laugh). Very often, too, their definitions obscure their subject-matter, and it is far harder to get any proper significance from them than in the thing which they intended to define. I am utterly incapable of saying whether that definition of Professor Flint's is an accurate definition of God or not. What I mean by "God," and perhaps Mr. Bradlaugh will take it as the best definition I can here give, is the source, whatever it be, of this metaphorical voice—of these intimations or monitions, that come to me in certain experiences which I have. Mr. Bradlaugh, of course, devoted much time to answering Professor Flint. He asked whether God was the source of that loyalty with which the Atheists he mentioned went to the stake, and I say from the bottom of my heart, that he was. God knows the Atheist though the Atheist knows not him. God is the source of loyalty of heart, in whomsoever it may be. If others are led to propound propositions which I believe to be false, and if they dispute other propositions which I believe to be true, do you think that God is going to judge them for that, so long as they have been true and faithful to their own reasoning powers (applause)? Mr. Bradlaugh noticed the phrase which fell from me, about a discussion like this being distasteful to me. I did not say that the matter under discussion was distasteful to me. I did not say that a discussion under other conditions would be distasteful to me. I did not say that it was at all distasteful to me to search the grounds of my own belief, for my own belief would be poor indeed were not such search my constant practice (hear, hear). Mr. Bradlaugh laid great stress, during the greater part of his speech, upon what appear to be, in different races and in different climes, the different and contradictory deliverances of conscience. That difficulty is one which has been felt by many persons, and dealt with, well and ill, by various writers. The difficulty is one of importance, and it arises, perhaps, from the word "conscience" being used in various different senses. My use of the word "conscience" is simply as being that voice of God (as I still call it) which says, "Do the right; don't do the wrong." It does not in anyway say what is right or what is wrong. That which I call the right, like so much of our manhood, is the gradual development and evolution of history, and it is largely dependent, as Mr. Bradlaugh says, upon climate and other external surroundings. We have to reason about what is right and wrong. We must have gradual education of the individual and of the race to get a clearer and more worthy conception of the right and wrong; and all I claim for conscience is that the man, having resolved in his own mind what is right and what is wrong, this conscience says, "Do the right, and do not the wrong." Therefore, in states of barbarous society, where misled reason has induced persons to think certain things were right which we look upon as crimes, still the voice of conscience must necessarily tell them to do the right. The thing is right to the individual if he thinks it right. It may be a terrible mistake of his—it may be a terrible mistake to believe or teach certain things; nevertheless, the voice of conscience says, "Do the right;" it does not define what the right is. That is one of the things which God leaves to be developed in humanity by slow degrees. Thank God, we see that the idea of the right and the wrong is purifying—is clarifying in the course of history. The conception of what is right and what is wrong is better now than it was a hundred years ago; the conception of what is right and what is wrong is better still than it was a thousand years ago. Many of the things then considered laudable are now considered base; and many of the things then considered base are now considered laudable. This voice of which I speak, however, like all other voices, may not be equally perceived at all times. Supposing that you were at school, and a certain bell rang at six o'clock every morning. If you accustom yourself to rising when the bell rings, you will naturally enough go on hearing it; but if you get into the habit of disregarding it, and turning over on the other side for another nap, the bell may sound loudly but you will cease to hear it. So it is, I take it, with the voice of God, which ever speaks—which ever pleads—but against which man may deafen himself. He may make himself so dull of understanding that he may not hear it clearly. Not only the individual man's own obstinacy may make him dull of hearing, but it must be conceded that this dulness of hearing may descend to him from long generations of those from whom he proceeds. It may be a part of his inheritance. But it does not follow that this voice does not exist, and that it does not still plead with him if he had the ear to hear it. No man is so lost but that if he strives to hear, that voice will become to him clearer and more clear. I ask you here whether you find any difficulty in deciding what, to you, is right or wrong? Mr. Bradlaugh is very fond of definitions. The words "right" and "wrong" are so simple that any definition of them would only obscure them. I know, and you know, what you mean by right and wrong. If I say of a thing, "That is not right, don't do it," you know what I mean. Can I speak in any plainer way than to say of a thing, "That is not right"? If there is no better way of explaining what you mean than this—if there is no plainer way—it is best not to attempt to define the word, because the definition would only tend to obscure it. Not being much accustomed to debates of this description, much of what I desired to say in the first half-hour was not said. I am told that all this experience which I have been trying to relate to you is fancy, and I am asked to prove that there is some being who can be imagined to be this God whom I believe I hear speaking to me. I might ask: "Is it not enough that not only do I think I hear this voice, but that so many hundreds and thousands of the great and good have also thought so? Is it not enough that many of the great reformers, many of the great leaders in the paths of righteousness and mercy, in this England of ours, tell us that they hear this voice? You must, if you deny it, either think they lie or that they are deluded. When Newman, Voysey, Theodore Parker—the glorious abolitionist of America—say that it is their most intimate experience, it is somewhat shallow to assert that there is nothing in it. I am not one of those who think that the existence of a God can be proved to the understanding of every one in a large audience on *à priori* grounds. At the same time the balance of probability on *à priori* grounds seems to be, to me, strongly in favour of Theism. I find that there is, in my own mental constitution, a demand for cause of some kind for every phenomenon. I want to know what has led to the phenomenon, and I find a good many other people are apt to inquire in the like direction. Even very little children, before they are sophisticated by us teachers and parsons, want to be informed as to the causes of things. Another point — I cannot help believing that all cause must be intelligent. Yes, I knew that would go down in Mr. Bradlaugh's notes; but I say again, I cannot conceive of any cause which is not intelligent in some sort of way (applause).

MR. BRADLAUGH: There are two things which are evidently quite certain so far as my opponent is concerned; one is that we shall have a good-tempered debate, and the other that we shall have a candid debate. Mr. Armstrong has said frankly, with reference to the definition of God, that he is perfectly incapable of saying whether the definition of Professor Flint is correct or not, and he has, I think I may say, complained that I am too fond of definitions. Will he permit me on this to read him an extract from Professor Max Müller's recent lecture: "It was, I think, a very good old custom never to enter upon the discussion of any scientific problem without giving beforehand definitions of the principal terms that had to be employed. A book on logic or grammar generally opened with the question, What is logic? What is grammar? No one would write on minerals without first explaining what he meant by a mineral, or on art, without defining, as well as he might, his idea of art. No doubt it was often as troublesome for the author to give such preliminary definitions as it seemed useless to the reader, who was generally quite incapable in the beginning of appreciating their full value. Thus it happened that the rule of giving verbal definitions came to be looked upon after a time as useless and obsolete. Some authors actually took credit for no longer giving these definitions, and it soon became the fashion to say that the only true and complete definition of what was meant by logic or grammar, by law or religion, was contained in the books themselves which treated of these subjects. But what has been the result? Endless misunderstandings and controversies which might have been avoided in many cases if both sides had clearly defined what they did and what they did not understand by certain words." I will show you presently where this need of accurate definition comes so very strongly. Mr. Armstrong is quite clear that he knows what right means; he is also quite clear that you know what he means. That may be true, but it also may not, and I will show you the difficulty. Suppose there were a thorough disciple, say of some bishop or church, who thought it right to put to death a man holding my opinions. That man would think the capital punishment for heresy right, Mr. Armstrong would not. That man's conscience would decide that it was right, Mr. Armstrong's would decide that it was not. What is the use of saying you both know what is right? The word right is a word by which you label certain things, thoughts, and actions, the rightness of which you have decided on some grounds known only to yourselves. It may be they are pleasant to you or disagreeable to your antagonist. I, in defining morality, gave you my reason for labelling the thing with the name "right." Mr. Armstrong has given you no reason whatever. Mr. Armstrong says that conscience is the voice of God which says: "Do that which is right, don't do that which is wrong." Yet the divine voice does not tell you what is right and what is wrong. Hence that conscience talking to the cannibal: "It is right to eat that man, he's tender; it's wrong to eat that man, he's tough"—(laughter)—and the voice of God says: "eat the tender men because it is right; don't eat the tough men because it is wrong." I ask how that illustration is to be dealt with? If the voice does not in any way enable you to determine the character of the act, then it simply means that what you call the voice of God asks you to continue committing every error which has been bequeathed you from past times as right, and to avoid every good thing because in past times it has been condemned and is yet condemned as wrong. If that is to be the conclusion, then I say that the voice of God is not a voice to be worshipped, and that it is not reasonable to worship such a voice; and taking that to be the definition I submit that upon that a negative answer must be given in this debate. Mr. Armstrong very frankly and candidly says that the conception of what is right and wrong is being cleared and purified day by day. That is, the conception now is different to what it was one hundred years ago, and better still than it was a thousand years ago; but the voice of God, a thousand years ago, told the Armstrong and Bradlaugh then living, to do that which conscience said to them was right, and which the conscience to-day says is wrong. Was God governed by the mis-education, the mis-information, and the mis-apprehension of the time? If the God was outside the ignorance of the day, why did he not set the people right? Was he powerless to do it? In which case, how do you make out that he is God? Or had he never the willingness to do it? In which case how do you make out that he was God good? And if he preferred to leave them in blindness, how do you reconcile that? Then we are told the voice is not always clear, but that you may make it more clear by a habit of obedience. That is so I suppose. And you may transmit the predisposition to the habit of galloping to horses on this side the ocean, the predisposition to the habit of trotting to horses on the other side the ocean; to thinking Mahommedanism in Turkey, and to thinking another "ism" in England, and some other "ism" in Hindustan. You do not transmit the actual thought any more than you transmit the actual gallop or trot, but you transmit the predisposition, given the appropriate surroundings to reproduce any action physical or mental. And the source of this is God, is it? I vow I do not understand how the Theist is to meet the contradiction thus involved. Then, Mr. Armstrong says that when he uses the word "right," he defies anyone to make it plainer. Let us see what that means: I forge a cheque; Mr. Armstrong says that's wrong. Why? Oh! it is a dishonest and dishonourable thing, it tends to injure, and so on. But let us see whether you are always quite clear about these things? When you are annexing a country, for example; praying to your God that you may annex successfully, and that he will protect you when you have annexed, does not your conscience run away with you, or does not God mislead you in some of these things? Is it not true that the moment you get outside the definition of the word "right," and the moment you say: "I have a standard of right which I will not tell you, because nothing I tell you will make it clear" you are launched at once into a heap of absurdities and contradictions? You think it is right to have one wife, the Turk thinks it right to have two. How are you to determine between them? It only means, that one of you has labelled bigamy "right" and the other has labelled it "wrong." You must have some kind of explanation to justify what you are talking about it. We had an argument offered by Mr. Armstrong which, if it meant anything, meant that the voice of the majority should prevail. Mr. Armstrong said, that it was not only his experience but that of thousands of others. Does he mean to tell me that problems of this kind are to be determined by an untrained majority, or by the verdict of a skilled minority? If by a majority, I have something to say to him, and if by the skilled minority, how are you to select them? In his first speech, which I did not quite finish replying to, we were told that God's peace and beauty were apprehended in lakes and mountains. But I have seen one lake—Michigan—the reverse of peace and beauty; I have seen little vessels knocked about by the waves, and dashed to pieces; and I have seen Mount Vesuvius when it has been the very opposite of calm and beautiful, and I have heard of the houses at Torre del Grecco—though I have never seen it—being burned in the night by the fiery lava stream. Where is the peace and beauty of that scene? You can take peace. Given a lake, and I can show you a tornado. Given a mountain and I can give you Vesuvius with the fiery stream burning the huts of the fishers on the slope of Torre del Grecco. Did God do this? Did God run the two vessels into one another on the Thames and have those hundreds of people drowned? If you take credit for the beauty you must also take debit for the pain and misery (applause). Well, then, I am told that religion is the noblest of all instincts. Max Müller tells us—whether that be true or not, as Francis Newman puts it—that religion is a word about which people never have agreed in any age of the world; about which there have been more quarrels than about any other word, and about which people have done more mischief than about any other word; and I will ask our friend to explain, if it be the noblest of all instincts, how is it that people have racked each other, and beheaded each other, and tortured each other by, or in the name of, this religion? We are told, and I am thankful to hear it, that we sceptics have purged it of a great deal of mischief, and we hope to do more in that way as we go on (applause). And here—and I want to speak with as much reverence as I can on the subject of prayer, and it is extremely difficult to touch upon it without giving my opponent pain—so I will deal with it as a general, and not a personal question. Mr. Armstrong said, after speaking of how he prayed against temptation : " He answered me as he has answered the immemorial prayer of Christendom and delivered me from temptation." Why does he not deliver from the temptation that misery, poverty, and ignorance bring to the little one who did not choose that he should be born in a narrow lane, or a back street, in an atmosphere redolent of squalor and filth ? This little one, whom God can lift out of temptation, but whom he lets still be cold and miserable, whom he sees famishing for food, him whom he sees go famishing to the baker's, watching to steal the loaf to relieve his hunger—why won't he deliver this little one? Does Mr. Armstrong say: "Oh, the little one must know how to pray before God will answer him"? Oh, but what a mockery to us that the source of all power places within the reach of the temptation—nay, puts as though surrounded by a mighty temptation trap, so that there should be no possible escape—that little one, and then gives way to the skilled entreaty, high tone, habit-cultured voice which Mr. Armstrong uses, while he is deaf to the rough pleading of the little one, and allows him to sink down, making no effort for his recovery! I have only one or two words more to say to you before I again finish, and I would use these to ask Mr. Armstrong to tell me what he meant by the word "cause," and what he meant by saying "cause must be intelligent"? By cause, I mean, all that without which an event cannot happen—the means towards an end, and by intelligence I mean the totality of mental ability—its activity and its results in each animal capable of it.

MR. ARMSTRONG: Mr. Bradlaugh has just been rebuking me for my laxness with respect to definitions, and has come down upon me with a great authority. Now, it is a habit of mine not to think much of authorities as authorities, but rather of the value of what they say. Mr. Bradlaugh came down upon me with Max Müller, and read a sentence in reference to the value of definitions, to the effect that they were wonderful things for preventing and avoiding controversies and disputes. Is it, I ask, Mr. Bradlaugh's experience that the number of definitions given from public platforms in his presence has tended to less controversy or to more? Has there been more or less talk with all these definitions, than there would have been without them? I fancied that Mr. Bradlaugh's career had been one very much connected with controversies, and that the definitions which he has been accustomed to give have not had the effect of leaving him in peace from controversy. I am perfectly amazed at Mr. Bradlaugh's memory, at the wonderful manner in which he manages to remember, with tolerable accuracy, what I have said, and to get down as he does the chief points of my speeches. I have, unfortunately, a miserable memory, although I have an excellent shorthand which I can write, and I cannot generally read it (laughter). Trusting, however, to those two guides, I must endeavour to reply. Mr. Bradlaugh unintentionally misrepresented me when he alleged that I had said that the voice of God, called conscience, was not always clear. I did not say that that voice was not always clear — what I said was that it was not always clearly heard. I illustrated this by the simile of the bell, the sound of which was perfectly clear of itself, but which was not heard by those who would not heed. Mr. Bradlaugh also accused me of going in for the authority of majorities, because I quoted a number of names and said that I might quote many more who concurred in the belief in Deity grounded upon the sort of experience which I said that I had myself enjoyed. Now, the *opinions* of the majority have no authority—at least they go for what they are worth, but are not a binding or an absolute authority. But the *experience* of a majority, or of a minority, or of a single individual, has authority. The experience of a single man is a fact, and all the rest of the world not having had that experience, or thinking that they have not had it, does not make it less the fact. Therefore, if you have half-a-dozen men upon whose words you can rely, who say that they have had a certain experience, because Mr. Bradlaugh says he has not had such experience, that makes it none the less the fact. Now I approach that awful question which stares in the face of the Theist—and which ioften seems to stare most cruelly—this question of the evil in the world. It is a question upon which the greatest intellects of mankind have broken themselves, one which has never been really explained or made clear, either by the Theist or the Atheist, but which is probably beyond the solution of the human faculties. All that we can do is to fringe the edge of the mystery, and to see whether the best feelings within us seem to guide us to anything approaching a solution. Do you think that these things of which Mr. Bradlaugh has spoken do not touch me as they touch him? Look, say, at the poor child born in misery, and living in suffering; it would absolutely break my heart if I thought that this could be the end of all. I believe that it would weigh me down so that I could not stand upon a public platform, or perform the ordinary business of life, if I believed that there were beings in the world of whom misery and sin were the beginning and the end. But I thank God that I am enabled to maintain my reason upon its seat, and my trust intact. I know, or I think I know, God as a friend. If he be a friend to me, shall he not be a friend to all? If I know by my own experience his wondrous loving kindness, can I not trust him for all the rest of the world, through all the ages of eternity? You may see a son who shall be familiar with his father's kindness, who shall always be kindly treated by his father; and there shall be a great warm love between them. But the child sees certain actions on the part of his father which he cannot explain. He beholds suffering apparently brought by his father upon others, and is, perhaps, inclined to rebel against his father's authority. But which is the truest child—the child who, having himself experienced his father's love, says: "Well, this is strange, it is a mystery; I would it were not so, but I know that my father is good, and will bring some good out of this which could not have been obtained otherwise;" or the child who says: "All my experience of my father's goodness shall go to the winds. I see a problem which I cannot explain, and I will, therefore, throw up my trust, rebel against the paternal goodness, and believe in my father's love no more!" It would be base in such of you as may be Atheisst to rest in such a trust, since you do not know the love of God; but were you touched with that love, this trust would come to you. It would come to you in your best and truest moments, the moments when you feel that you are most akin with all that is good and holy, and when you feel, as it were, lifted above what is base. This problem of the evil in the world, I have said, surpasses the faculties of humanity to solve, either from the platform of the Theist, the Atheist, or the Pantheist. I ask you what you conceive to be the highest good to humanity? Is not the highest good, virtue? You say, it may be, happiness is better. Take the Huguenot. One way, with him, led to happiness, the other to destruction. Was the choice he made the better or the worse? You say the better? Then you hold that virtue is better than happiness. With regard to virtue, imagine, if you can, a world free from every sort of suffering, from every sort of temptation, every sort of trial, what a very nice world to live in, but what very poor creatures we should all be! Where would be virtue, where valour, where greatness, where nobility, where would be all those high functions which call forth our reverence, and make us look up from men to the God of man? The world is not made of sugar-plums. I, for my own part, cannot conceive how virtue, the highest good which we can conceive, could possibly come about in human character unless human character had evil against which it had to contend (applause). If you can tell me how we could have a world in which men should be great, and good, and chivalrous, and possess all such qualities as raise feelings of reverence in our bosoms, where nevertheless all should be smooth and easy, you will have told me of something which, I think, has never been told to any human being (applause).

Mr. BRADLAUGH: A large number of definitions lead to more controversy or to less. If the definitions are offered to the minds of people well educated, and thoroughly understanding them—to much less controversy and to more accuracy; and when they are offered to people who are yet ignorant, and have yet to understand them, then they lead to more controversy, but even there, also, to more accuracy. I am asked: Can you tell me how to make a world? I cannot. Do you intend to base your conclusions on my ignorance? If there be an *onus*, it lies on you, not on me. It is your business to show that the maker you say ought to be adored, has made the world as good as it can be. It is not my business at all to enter upon world-making. Then

I am not sure—while I am quite ready to be set right upon a verbal inaccuracy—I am not sure there is very much distinction between the voice not being heard, and not being clearly heard. It is said to be the voice of God that speaks; but he made the deafness or otherwise of the person to whom he speaks, or he is not the creator, preserver, "the dearest friend in whom I trust, on whom I rely"—these are Mr. Armstrong's words. If God cannot prevent the deafness, then the reliance is misplaced; if he made the deafness, it is of no use that he is talking plainly; if he has made the person too deaf to hear his voice, then the voice is a mockery. Then I had it put to me, that the opinions of majorities were not binding as authority; they only had their value as expressions of opinion; but that the experiences of individuals are binding. What does that mean? Is there such a certitude in consciousness that there can be no mistake in experience? What do you mean? When you have a notion you have had an experience, and I have a notion you have not had it? Supposing, for example, a man says: "I have experience of a room which raced with the Great Northern train to London; it was an ordinary room, with chairs and tables in it, and none of them were upset, and it managed to run a dead heat with the Great Northern express." You would say: "My good man, if you are speaking seriously, you are a lunatic." "No," he would say, "that is my experience." Mr. Armstrong says that that experience deserves weight. I submit not unless you have this: that the experience must be of facts coming within the possible range of other people's experience; and must be experience which is testable by other people's experience, with an ability on the part of the person relating to clearly explain his experience, and that each phenomenon he vouches to you, to be the subject possible of criticism on examination by yourself, and that no experience which is perfectly abnormal, and which is against yours, has any weight whatever with you, or ought to have, except, perhaps, as deserving examination. When it possibly can be made part of your experience, yes; when it admittedly cannot be made part of your experience, no. A man with several glasses of whisky sees six chandeliers in this room; that is his experience—not mine. I do not refuse to see; I cannot see more than three. Mr. Armstrong says the problem of evil never has been made clear by Atheist or Theist. There is no burden on us to make it clear. The burden is upon the person who considers that he has an all-powerful friend of loving kindness, to show how that evil exists in connection with his statement that that friend could prevent it. If he will not prevent it, he is not of that loving kindness which is pretended. Mr. Armstrong says: "My dear friend is kind to me, shall I not believe that he is kind to the little lad who is starving?" What, kind to the lad whom he leaves unsheltered and ill-clad in winter, whose mother is drunken because the place is foul, whose father has been committed to gaol? Where is the evidence to that lad of God's loving kindness to him? God, who stands by whilst the little child steals something; God, who sets the policeman to catch him, knowing he will go amongst other criminals, where he will become daily the more corrupted; God, who tells him from the Bench through the mouth of the justice, that he has given way to the temptation of the devil, when it is the very God has been the almighty devil (applause). That may be a reason for Mr. Armstrong adoring his friend, but it is no reason for this poor boy to adore. "Ah," Mr. Armstrong says, "my reason for homage is this. I should be dissatisfied if this were going to last for ever, or if this were to be the whole of it; that is so bad I should be in anguish were there no recompense." You condemn it if it is to continue. How can you worship the being who allows that even temporarily which your reason condemns? Has he marked his right to be adored as God by the little girl who is born of a shame-marked mother in the shadow of the workhouse walls, who did not select the womb from which she should come, and whose career, consequent on her birth, is one of shame and perhaps crime too. Ah! that friend you love, how his love is evidenced to that little girl is yet to be made clear to me. Then comes another problem of thought which I am not sure I shall deal fairly with. Is the highest good virtue or happiness? But the highest happiness is virtue. That act is virtuous which tends to the greatest happiness of the greatest number, and which inflicts the least injury on any—that which does not so result in this is vice. When you put happiness and virtue as being utterly distinguished, in your mind they may be so, but not in my mind. You have confused the definition of morality which I gave on the first opening; you have, without explaining it, substituted another in lieu of it. You would be right to say my definition is wrong, and give another definition, but you have no right to ignore my definition and use my word in precisely the opposite sense to that in which I used it. A very few words now will determine this question for this evening, and I will ask you to remember the position in which we are here. I am Atheist, our friend is Theist. He has told you practically that the word "God" is incapable of exact definition, and if this is so, then it is incapable of exact belief. If it is incapable of exact definition, it is incapable of exact thought. If thought is confused you may have prostration of the intellect, and this is all you can have. Our friend says that he prays and that his prayer is answered daily, but he forgot the millions of prayers to whom God is deaf. In his peaceful mountains and lakes—Vesuvius and Lake Michigan escaped him. The fishers in Torre del Grecco, they on whom the lava stream came down in the night, had their lips framed no cry for mercy? Did not some of those hundreds who were carried to death on the tide of the muddy Thames, did not they call out in their despair? and yet he was deaf to them. He listened to you, but it is of those to whom he did not listen of whom I have to speak. If he listens to you and not to them he is a respecter of persons. He may be one for you to render homage to, but not for me. First, then, the question is: "Is it reasonable to worship God?" and the word "worship" has been left indistinctly defined. I defy anyone who has listened to Mr. Armstrong to understand how much or how little he would exclude or include in worship. I made it clear how much I would include. Our friend has said nothing whatever relating to the subject with which we have had to deal.. His word "God" has been left utterly undefined; the words "virtue" and "happiness," and the words "right" and "wrong," are left equally unexplained; the questions I put to him of cause and intelligence have been left as though they were not spoken. I do not make this a reproach to him, because I know it is the difficulty of the subject with which he has to deal. The moment you tell people what you mean, that moment you shiver the Venetian glass which contains the liquor that is not to be touched. I plead under great difficulty. I plead for opinions that have been made unpopular; I appeal for persons who, in the mouths of their antagonists, often have associated with them all that is vicious. It is true that Mr. Armstrong has no such reproach. He says that God will only try me by that judgment of my own reason, and he makes my standard higher than God's on the judgment day. God made Bruno; do you mean that Bruno's heresy ranks as high as faith, and that Bruno at the judgment will stand amongst the saints? This may be high humanity, but it is no part of theology. Our friend can only put it that because in his own goodness he makes an altar where he can worship, and a church where he would make a God kind and loving as himself, and that as he is ready to bless his fellows, so must his God be; but he has shown no God for me to worship, and he has made out no reasonableness to worship God except for himself, to whom, he says, God is kind. Alas! that so many know nothing of his kindness (applause). I beg to move the thanks of this meeting to Mr. Rothera for presiding this evening.

Mr. ARMSTRONG: I wish to second that.

Carried unanimously.

The CHAIRMAN: Permit me just to express the obligations I feel under to you for having made my duty so simple and pleasant. My position as chairman necessarily and properly excludes me from making any judgment whatever upon the character and quality of what has been addressed to you. Notwithstanding that, I may say this: that it is, I believe, a healthy sign of the times when a number of men and women, such as have met together in this room, can listen to such addresses as have been made tonight, for it will help on our civilisation. And if you want a definition of what is right, I say that our business is to learn what is true, then we shall do what is right (applause).

SECOND NIGHT.

THE CHAIRMAN, who was much applauded, said: Ladies and Gentlemen—It is with much satisfaction that I resume my duties as chairman this evening. No one occupying this position could fail to be gratified with the high tone and excellent temper of the debate which we listened to last night (hear, hear), or, in noting as I did, the earnest, sustained, and intelligent attention of a large and much over-crowded audience (applause). I regard this as a healthful sign of the times. There are those who look upon such a discussion as this as dangerous and irreverent. I do not share in that opinion (hear, hear). There is an intelligence abroad that no longer permits men to cast the burden of their beliefs upon mere authority, but which compels them to seek for reasons for the faith that is in them (hear, hear). To those, I think, such discussion as this, maintained in the spirit of last evening, cannot fail to be useful. It is obvious that the first requisite of religion is, that it be true. Fear of the results of investigation, therefore, should deter no one from inquiry. That which is true in religion, cannot be shaken, and that which is false no one should desire to preserve (applause). Now, as you are aware, Mr. Armstrong in this discussion is charged with the duty of maintaining the proposition that it is reasonable in us to worship God. The negative of that proposition is supported by Mr. Bradlaugh. Under the arrangement for the debate, Mr. Bradlaugh is tonight entitled to half-an-hour for his opening, Mr. Armstrong to half-an-hour for his reply. After that a quarter-hour will be given to each alternately, until Mr. Armstrong will conclude the debate at ten o'clock. I have now great pleasure in asking Mr. Bradlaugh to open the discussion (applause).

MR. BRADLAUGH, who was very warmly received, said: In contending that it is not reasonable to worship God, it seemed to me that I ought to make clear to you, at any rate, the words I used, and the sense in which I used them, and to do that I laid before you last night several definitions, not meaning that my definitions should necessarily bind Mr. Armstrong, but meaning that, unless he supplied some other and better explanations for the words, the meaning I gave should be, in each case, taken to be my meaning all through. I did not mean that he was to be concluded by the form of my definition if he were able to correct it, or if he were able to give a better instead; but I think I am now entitled to say that he ought to be concluded by my definitions, and this, from the answer he has given (hear, hear). The answer was frank—very frank—(hear) and I feel reluctant to base more upon it than I ought to do in a discussion conducted as this has been. If I were meeting an antagonist who strove to take every verbal advantage, I might be tempted to pursue only the same course; but when I find a man speaking with evident earnestness, using language which seems to be the utter abandonment of his cause, I would rather ask him whether some amendment of the language he used might not put his case in a better position. His declaration was that he was perfectly incapable of saying whether the definition, which I had taken from Professsor Flint, of God, was correct or not (hear, hear). Now, I will ask him, and you, too, to consider the consequence of that admission. No definition whatever is given by him of the word "God." There was not even the semblance, or attempt of it. The only words we got which were akin to a definition, except some words which, it appears, I took down hastily, and which Mr. Armstrong abandoned in his next speech, the only words bearing even the semblance of a definition, are "an awful inscrutable somewhat" (laughter and hear, hear). Except these words, there have been no words in the arguments and in the speeches of Mr. Armstrong which enabled me, in any fashion, to identify any meaning which he may have of it, except phrases which contradict each other as soon as you examine them (applause). Now, what is the definition of which Mr. Armstrong says that he is incapable of saying whether or not it is correct? "That God is a self-existent, eternal being, infinite in power and wisdom, and perfect in holiness and goodness, the maker of heaven and earth." Now, does Mr. Armstrong mean that each division of the definition comes within his answer? Does he mean that in relation to no part of that which is predicated in this definition is he capable of saying whether it is correct or not? Because, if he does, he is answered by his own speech, as a portion of this defines God as being perfect in holiness and goodness, in power and wisdom; and it defines him as eternal in duration and infinite in his existence; and also defines him as being the creator of the universe. Now, if Mr. Armstrong means that "as a whole, I can't say whether it is correct or not," or if, in defending his position, he means that, having divided the definition in its parts, he cannot say whether it is, in any one part, correct or not, then I must remind him that, in this debate, the onus lies upon him of saying what it is he worships, and what it is he contends it is reasonable of us to worship (hear, hear). If he cannot give us a clear and concise notion of what he worships, and of what he says it is reasonable for us to worship, I say that his case has fallen to the ground. It must be unreasonable to worship that of which you, in thought, cannot predicate anything in any way —accurately or inaccurately (applause). Mr. Armstrong evidently felt—I hope that you will not think that the feeling was justified—that there was a tendency on my part to make too much of, and to be too precise as to, the meaning of words used. Permit me to say it is impossible to be too precise; it is impossible to be too clear; it is impossible to be too distinct—(hear, hear)—especially when you are discussing a subject in terms which are not used by everybody in the same sense, and which are sometimes not used by the mass of those to whom you are addressing yourself at all (applause). It is still more necessary to be precise when many of those terms have been appropriated by the teachers of different theologies and mythologies, such teachers having alleged that the use of the words meant something which, on the face of it, contradicted itself, and by other teachers who, if they have not been self-contradictory, have attached meanings widely different to those given by their fellows (hear, hear). I will ask you, then, to insist with me that what is meant by God should be given us in such words that we can clearly and easily identify it (hear, hear). If you cannot even in thought identify God, it is unreasonable—absolutely unreasonable—to talk of worshipping "it" (applause). What is "it" you are going to worship? Can you think clearly what it is you are going to worship? If you can think clearly for yourself what it is, tell me in what words you think it. It may be that my brain may not be skilled enough to fully comprehend that, but, at any rate, we shall then have an opportunity of testing for ourselves how little or how much clear thought you may have on the subject (laughter and applause). If you are obliged to state that it is impossible to put your thoughts in words so clear and so distinct that I may understand the meaning of it as clearly as you do, or that a person of ordinary capacity cannot comprehend the words in which you describe it—if that is impossible, then it is unreasonable to ask me to worship it (loud applause). I say it is unreasonable to ask me to worship an unknown quantity —an unrecognisable symbol expressing nothing whatever. If you know what it is you worship—if you think you know what it is you worship—I say it is your duty to put into words what you think you know (hear, hear). We have had in this debate some pleas put forward, which, if they had remained unchallenged, might have been some sort of pleas for the existence of a Deity, but each of those pleas has in turn failed. I do not want to use too strong a phrase, so I will say that each in turn has been abandoned. Take, for instance, the plea of beauty, harmony, and calmness of the world, as illustrated by lakes and mountains, to which I contrasted storms and volcanoes. Mr. Armstrong's reply to that was: "But this involves problems which are alike insoluble by Theist and Atheist." If it is so, why do you worship what is non-capable of solution? If there be no solution, why do you put that word "God" as representative of the solution which you say is unattainable, and ask me to prostrate myself before it and adore it? (applause). We must have consistency of phraseology. Either the problem is soluble—then the onus is upon you to state it in reasonable terms; or it is insoluble, and then you have abandoned the point you set out to prove, because it must be unreasonable to worship an insoluble proposition (applause). How do you know anything of that God you ask us to worship? I must avow that, after listening carefully to what has fallen from Mr. Armstrong, I have been unable to glean what he knows of God or how he knows it (hear, hear). I remember he has said something about a "voice of God," but he has frankly admitted that the voice in question has spoken differently and in contradictory senses in different ages (loud cries of "no, no,")—and those who say "no," will do better to leave Mr. Armstrong to answer for himself as to the accuracy of what I state (hear, hear). I say he frankly admitted that the voice he alluded to had spoken differently and contradictorily in different ages. (Renewed

cries of " no "). I say yes, and I will give the evidence of
my yes. (Cries of " no, no," " order," and " hear, hear.")
I say yes, and I will give the evidence of my yes (hear,
hear, and applause). Mr. Armstrong said that in one
hundred years there had been a purification, and an
amelioration, and a clearing away; and that that change
had been vaster still since one thousand years ago (applause). He is responsible for admitting what I said
about the definition of morality being different in one
age and amongst one people to what it is in another
age and amongst another people; and if that does not mean
exactly what I put substantially to you, it has no meaning
at all (loud applause). I strive not to misrepresent
that which I have to answer; I will do my best to understand what it is that is urged against me. Those who hold
a different judgment should try, at least, to suspend it until I
have finished (hear, hear, and applause). In the Baird
Lectures, to which I referred last night—and let me here
say that I don't think that any complaint can be fairly made
of my quoting from them—something was said last night
about my using great men as an authority. Now I do not do
that; but if I find that a man, whose position and learning
gave him advantages with regard to a subject upon which
I am speaking, and he has expressed what I wished to say
better than I can do—if I use his language it is right
I should say from where I have taken my words (hear, hear)
And if I remember right, we had, last night, quotations from
Charles Voysey, Professor Newman, Professor Blackie, and
a host of similar writers on the other side. I take it they
were given in the same fashion that I intended in giving the
names of the writers of the quotations I have cited—not for
the purpose of overwhelming me with their authority, but
simply to inform me and you from whence were got the
words used (hear, hear). Now, Professor Flint, in his book
on Atheism, directed against the position taken up by men
like myself, says : " The child is born, not into the religion
of nature but into blank ignorance; and, if left entirely to
itself, would probably never find out as much religious truth
as the most ignorant of parents can teach it." Again, on page
23 he says : " The belief that there is one God, infinite in
power, wisdom, and goodness, has certainly not been
wrought out by each one of us for himself, but has been
passed on from man to man, from parent to child: tradition, education, common consent, the social medium, have

exerted great influence in determining its acceptance and prevalence." Now, what I want to put to you from this is that, just as Max Müller and others have done, you must try to find out whether what is to be understood by the word " God " is to be worshipped or not, by tracing backwards the origin and growth of what is to-day called religion. You will have to search out the traditions of the world, should there fail to be any comprehensible meaning come from the other side. Now, what God is it that we are to worship? Is it the Jewish God? Is it the Mahometan God? Is it the God of the Trinitarian Christian? Is it one of the gods of the Hindus? Or is it one of the gods of the old Greeks or Italians, and, if so, which of them? And in each case from what source are we to get an accurate definition of either of those gods? Perhaps Mr. Armstrong will say that it is none of these. He will probably decline to have any of these Gods fastened upon him as the proper God to worship; but the very fact that there are so many different gods—different with every variety of people—contradictory in their attributes and qualities—the very fact that there is a wide difference in believers in a God makes it but right that I should require that the God we are asked to worship should be accurately defined (applause). In the current number of the *Contemporary Review*, Professor Monier Williams, dealing with the development of Indian religious thought, has a paragraph which is most appropriate to this debate. He says, on page 246: " The early religion of the Indo-Aryans was a development of a still earlier belief in man's subjection to the powers of nature and his need of conciliating them. It was an unsettled system, which at one time assigned all the phenomena of the universe to one first Cause; at another, attributed them to several Causes operating independently; at another, supposed the whole visible creation to be a simple evolution from an eternal creative germ. It was a belief which, according to the character and inclination of the worshipper was now monotheism, now tritheism, now polytheism, now pantheism. But it was not yet idolatry. Though the forces of nature were thought of as controlled by divine persons, such persons were not yet idolised. There is no evidence from the Vedic hymns that images were employed. The mode of divine worship continued to be determined from a consideration of human liking and dislikings. Every worshipper praised the gods

because he liked to be praised himself. He honoured them with offerings because he liked to receive presents himself. This appears to have been the simple origin of the sacrificial system, afterwards closely interwoven with the whole religious system. And here comes the difficult question—What were the various ideas expressed by the term sacrifice? In its purest and simplest form it denoted a dedication of some simple gift as an expression of gratitude for blessings received. Soon the act of sacrifice became an act of propitiation for purely selfish ends. The favour of celestial beings who were capable of conferring good or inflicting harm on crops, flocks, and herds, was conciliated by offerings and oblations of all kinds. First, the gods were invited to join their worshippers at the every-day meal. Then they were invoked at festive gatherings, and offered a share of the food consumed. Their bodies were believed to be composed of ethereal particles, dependent for nourishment on the indivisible elementary essence of the substances presented to them, and to be furnished with senses capable of being gratified by the aroma of butter and grain offered in fire (homa) ; and especially by the fumes arising from libations of the exhilarating juice extracted from the Soma plant."
I will allege that you cannot give me a definition of God that does not originate in the ignorance of man as to the causes of phenomena which are abnormal to him, and which he cannot explain. The wonderful, the extraordinary, the terrific, the mysterious, the mighty, the grand, the furious, the good, the highly beneficent—all these that he did not understand became to him God. He might have understood them on careful investigation had his mind then been capable for the search, but instead of that he attributed them to huge personifications of the Unknown—the word behind which to-day is God, and it is the equivalent for all he observed, but did not comprehend, for all that happened of which he knew not the meaning (applause). It was not education but ignorance which gave birth to the so-called idea of a God (hear, hear). And I will submit to you that, in truth, all forms of worship have arisen from exaggeration and misapplication of what men have seen in their fellow-men and fellow-women. A man found that a big furious man might be pacified and calmed by soothing words ; that a big avaricious man might be satisfied and pleased with plenteous gifts ; that this one might be compelled to do something by

angry words or harsh treatment; and that this one could be won by supplications to comply with his wishes—and what he imagined or observed as to his fellows he applied to the unknown, thinking, no doubt, that that which he had found efficacious in the known experience, might also be efficacious in that in which he had no experience. And what did you find? You found the sailor at sea, who did not understand navigation, offering candles to his Deity, or special saint, and promising more offerings of a similar character if the Deity brought him safe into port. I say it is more reasonable to teach him how to steer than how to worship, and also more reasonable to know something about the science of navigation. That would prove much more serviceable than worship, for when he relied upon candles, he ran upon rocks and reefs, but as soon as he understood navigation, he could bring his own ship safely into port (applause). Prayer is spoken of by Mr. Armstrong as an act of worship. What does it imply? It implies a belief held on the part of the person who prays, that he may be noticed by the being to whom he prays; and it also implies that he is asking that being to do something which he would have left undone but for that prayer. Then does he think that he can influence the person whom he addresses by his rank or by his position? Does he think he can influence his Deity by his emotion? Does he think that as he would win a woman's love, so he would gain God, by passionate devotion? Does he think that, as he would frighten a man, so he would influence God through fear? Does he appeal to God's logic, or to his pity? Does he appeal to his mercy or to his justice? or does he hope to tell God one thing he could not know without the prayer? (loud applause.) I want an answer, here, clear and thorough, from one who says that prayer is a reasonable worship to be offered to God (renewed applause). Something was said last night about a cause being necessarily intelligent, and I think, in my speech afterwards, I challenged the assertion. Nothing was said to explain what was meant, nothing was done to further explain the matter, and although I defined what I meant by cause, and defined what I meant by intelligence, no objection was taken. Now, I have seen a hut crushed by an avalanche falling on it, as I have been crossing the Alps. Does Mr. Armstrong mean to tell me that the avalanche which crushed the hut was intelligent, or that it had an intelligent wielder? If the avalanche is intelligent, why does he think so? If the avalanche has an intelligent wielder, please explain to me the goodness of that intelligent wielder who dashes the avalanche on the cottage? (applause). If you tell me that it is a mystery which you cannot explain, I say it is unreasonable to ask me to worship such a mystery—(renewed applause)—and as long as you call it a mystery, and treat it as that which you cannot explain, so long you have no right to ask me to adore it. There was a time when man worshipped the lightning and thunder, and looked upon them as Deity. But now he has grown wiser, and, having investigated the subject, instead of worshipping the lightning as a Deity, he erects lightning-conductors and electric wires, and chains the lightning and thunder God; knowledge is more potent than prayer (applause). As long as they were worshipped science could do nothing, but now we see to what uses electricity has been brought. When they knew that the lightning-conductor was more powerful than the God they worshipped, then science was recognised the mighty master and ruler, instead of ignorant faith (applause). I have already submitted that there has not been the semblance of proof or authority for the existence of any being identifiable in words to whom it would be reasonable to offer worship, and I will show you the need for pressing that upon you. A strong statement was made last night which amounted to an admission that there was wrong here which should not be, and that, but for the hope on the part of the speaker that that wrong would be remedied at some future time, he would be in a state of terrible despair. He gave no reason for the hope, and no evidence why he held the hope. He only contended that things were so bad here that they would be indefensible except for the hope that they would be remedied. This admission is fatal to the affirmation of God to be worshipped in the way here mentioned. Then we had something said about experience. All experience must be experience of the senses : you can have no other experience whatever. To quote again from Max Müller: "All consciousness begins with sensuous perception, with what we feel, and hear, and see. Out of this we construct what may be called conceptual knowledge, consisting of collective and abstract concepts. What we call thinking consists simply in addition and subtraction of precepts and concepts. Conceptual knowledge differs from sensuous knowledge, not in substance, but in form only. As far as the material is concerned, nothing exists in the intellect except what existed before in the senses." It is the old proposition put in different forms by Locke, Spinoza, and others, over and over again, but it has to be taken with this qualification that you have innumerable instances of hallucinations of the senses. Delusions on religious matters are open to the remark that of all hallucinations of the senses—as Dr. H. Maudsley shows in the *Fortnightly Review*—of all hallucinations of the senses those on religious matters only keep current with the religious teachings of the day. Sight, touch, smell, hearing, feeling—all are the subject of illusion as is shown over and over again. Any man bringing as evidence to us the report of experience which is only of an abnormal character, is bound to submit it to a test which is something beyond in severity that which we should apply to normal events. The more abnormal it is the more particularity in detail do I wish, in order to examine it, so that I may be able to identify it; and the more curious the statement the more carefully do I wish to test it. Loose words in theology will not do, and here I submit that at present we stand, with, at any rate, on one side, nothing whatever affirmed against me. I gathered last night—I hope incorrectly—I gathered last night—I hope the words were spoken incautiously—that Mr. Armstrong held it to be natural that a man should have to struggle against wrong, vice, and folly, for the purpose of bringing out the higher qualities, and that it was alleged that it was to that struggle we were indebted for our virtue. If that were a real thought on the part of Mr. Armstrong it is but a sorry encouragement to any attempts at reformation and civilisation. Why strive to remove misery and wrong if the struggle against them is conducive to virtue? It would take a long time to bring about any ameliorating change in society if such doctrine were widely held (loud applause).

The Rev. R. A. ARMSTRONG, who was applauded on rising, said: Mr. Chairman and Friends—I wish, in justice to myself, to say that I freely offered Mr. Bradlaugh the choice of parts as to the order of speaking. I know not which way the balance of advantage lies; but after the speech we have listened to, I think you will agree with me that he who speaks first the second night has a considerable pull (laughter). Last night as I passed down that awful flight of stairs, which they must climb who, in this town, would soar from the nether world to the celestial realms of Secularism, I heard many comments, and among others one man just behind me said: "Oh! Armstrong is nowhere in Bradlaugh's hands. Bradlaugh can do just what he likes with him" (laughter). Now, my friend said the very truth in a certain sense. As a debater I am nowhere compared with Mr. Bradlaugh. He has fluency—I compute that in thirty minutes I can string together some 4,000 words, while, I fancy, Mr. Bradlaugh's score would be just about 6,000—so that to equalise our mere mechanical advantages I ought really to have three minutes to every two of his. If I have omitted many things which I ought to have said, it is due to this reason (laughter and hear, hear)—for I have not been silent during the time assigned to me. Of course, I do not complain of this. Then, to say nothing of Mr. Bradlaugh's powerful intellect, to which I do not pretend, and his wide reading, he is in constant practice at this work so new to me, so much so that I find almost every thought he expressed last night, and in almost—sometimes precisely—identical language, printed in his pamphlets, and much of it even spoken in one or other o his numerous debates. Take this, along with his prodigious memory, and you will see that the doctrine of Atheism has, indeed, in him, the very ablest defender that its friends could wish. And if what he says is not enough to demolish Theism, then you may be sure that Theism cannot be demolished (applause). But then, friends, I do want you not to look on this as a personal struggle between Mr. Bradlaugh and myself at all. I no more accept it in that light than I would accept a challenge from him to a boxing match, and I think you will all agree with me that in that case, in discretion I should show the better part of valour (hear, hear, and laughter). We are both speaking in all earnestness of what we hold to be the truth. Neither of us, I presume, in the least, expects to make converts on the spot: converts so quickly made would be like enough to be swayed back the other way next week. But we do desire that the seed of our words should sink into your minds; that you should give them your reverent attention, that, in due season, so far as they are good and true, they may ripen into matured convictions of the truth (applause). And now let me look back at the position in which this conference was left last night. I am the more at liberty to do so, as to-night Mr. Bradlaugh has only—or chiefly—done two things, namely, repeated some things which he said last night, and answered certain arguments of Professor Flint. That is perfectly fair, but it is equally fair for me to leave Professor Flint to answer for himself (hear hear, and applause). And I complain that Mr. Bradlaugh either did not listen to, or did not understand, what I endeavoured to put in plainest words about the function of that voice of God which we call conscience (hear, hear). Observe, that while in different climes and ages, ay, in the same man at different times, the conceptions of the particular deeds that come under the head of right differ, the idea of rightness itself, of rectitude, is always and invariably the same, from its first faint glimmer in the savage little removed comparatively from the lower animal, from which he is said to be developed, to the season of its clear shining, luminous and glorious, in hero, prophet, martyr, saint—in Elizabeth Fry, in Mary Carpenter, in Florence Nightingale. To speak metaphysically, the abstract subjective idea of right is the same and one, but our ideas of the concrete and objective right develop and progress ever towards a purer and more beautiful ideal. We have by our own powers to satisfy ourselves as best we can what is right. But when we have made up our minds, the voice of God sounds clear as a bell upon the soul and bids us do it (applause). This I stated again and again last night, yet to-night again Mr. Bradlaugh has confounded the two things. Mr. Bradlaugh raised a laugh with his story of the cannibal objecting to the tough, and choosing the tender meal. That cannibal, in so far, does but illustrate how a man is swayed by those lower instincts and desires which I rigorously and definitely distinguished and separated from conscience. Why Mr. Bradlaugh confounded this with a case of the deliverance of conscience I cannot think, because I am so sure it was neither to make you grin nor to confuse your minds (hear, hear). The latter part of the first night's debate turned on the mystery of evil. But Mr. Bradlaugh did not then venture to allege the possibility of a world in which noble character could be developed without the contact with suffering and pain (hear, hear). He said he was not called upon to make a world; happily not; but at any rate he should not question the excellence of the world in which he lives unless he can at least conceive a better—(loud applause)—and I say that where evil had never been, or what we call evil, manliness, bravery, generosity, sympathy, tenderness, could never be (applause). A world without temptation would be a world without virtue (hear, hear). A world all pleasurable would be a world without goodness, and even the pleasurable itself would cease by sheer monotony to give any pleasure at all. A world not developed out of the conflict of good and evil, or joy and pain, would necessarily be an absolutely neutral world, without emotion of any sort. Unless the whole tint is to be neutral, you must have light and shade; and the only test by which to judge whether the power controlling the world is good or evil—God or Devil, as Mr. Bradlaugh says— (applause)—is to note whether light or darkness preponderates; and not only that, but whether the movement, the tendency, the development, the drift of things is towards the gradual swallowing up of darkness by the light, or light by darkness; whether freedom, happiness, virtue, are in the procession of the ages losing their ground, or slowly, surely winning ever fresh accession (applause). I take it, then, that if we are to have a final predominance of goodness—nay, even of happiness, if you make that the highest good—it can only be by these things winning their way by degrees out of the evil which is their shadow. And I invite you once more to test this from experience. My own experience, clear and sure, and that of every other devout man, is simply this: that whatever sorrow, whatever pain we suffer, though it wring our very heart, the time is sure to come when, looking back thereon, we thank God that it was given us, perceiving that it was good, not evil, that befel us, being the means, in some way or other, of our further advance in happiness or goodness, or nearness to our heavenly Father. You tell me it is all very well for me; but you point to those whose lot is cast in less pleasant places, and ask me what of them? Is God good to them? Well, I will take you to a dark and dismal cellar beneath the reeking streets of a mighty city. And this picture is not drawn from fancy, it is a photograph from the life of one I know of. In that dark and poor abode you shall enter, and you shall see an aged woman to whom that spot is home. She is eaten up with disease, the inheritance, doubtless, of her forefathers' sin. For fifty years her simple story has been of alternations between less pain and more. Beside her are two orphan children, no kith or kin of hers, but adopted by her out of the large love which she nurtures in her heart, to share the pence she wins from the mangle, every turn of which is, to her, physical pain. Well, surely, she knows nought of God, has none of those "experiences" which Mr. Bradlaugh treats as if they were luxuries confined to the comfortable Theist in his easy-chair, or on his softly-pillowed bed. Ay, but she is rising from her knees to turn to the dry crust on the board, which is all she has to share with the children. And what says she as you enter? "Oh, sir, I was only thanking God for his goodness, and teaching these poor children so." Now, if Mr. Bradlaugh is right in declaring we can know nought of God, then that old woman ought never to have eased her laden heart by the outburst of her prayer, ought to have cast out of her as a freak of lunacy the peace that stole upon her there as she rose from her knees, ought to have shunned teaching those children, whose lot was like to be as hard as hers, one word about the reliance that she had on God (applause). Instead of that she taught the prosperous man who stumbled down the broken stair into her abode, a lesson of trust and faith in the goodness and presence of God, which he never forgot as long as he lived (hear, hear and applause). I sat the other day beside a dying girl. Her body was in hideous pain, but her face was lit with a light of beauty and of love which told a wondrous tale of her spirit's life. She died, and her mother and her sisters weep to-day. But a new love, a new gentleness, a new sense of the nearness of the spirit-world has already blossomed in their home, and, I am not sure that they would call her back even if their voices could avail. So it is; this woe which we call evil is the sacred spring of all that is beautiful and good (hear, hear). To the Atheist the world's sorrow must, indeed, be insupportable. If he be sincere and have a heart, I do not know how he can ever eat and drink and make merry, still less how he can make a jest and raise a titter in the very same speech in which he dwells with all the skill of practised eloquence upon that woe (applause). If I were an Atheist I hardly think I could ever throw off the darkness of this shadow. But, believing in God, whom I personally know, and know as full of love, I am constrained to trust that, though this evil be a mystery the full significance of which I cannot understand, and though relatively to the little sum of things here and now it seem great, yet that relatively to the whole plan and sum of the universe it is very small, and that that poor child, born of sin and shame, who knew no better than to steal the loaf, shall one day wear a diadem of celestial glory, and be by no means least in the Kingdom of Heaven. And when I see the Atheist smiling, laughing, having apparently a light heart in him, I am bound to suppose that he too, somehow, trusts that goodness and happiness are going to win in the end—that is, that goodness is the ultimately overruling power. And if he believes that, he believes in the power which men call God (applause). Now, Mr. Bradlaugh has castigated me with some severity for not obliging him with definitions. It is impossible, he says, to be too precise in the use of words, and I agree with him. But by definitions I cannot make the simplest words in the English language more plain to you (hear, hear). He, himself, has given us some specimens of definitions which I do not think have made things much clearer than they were before. There are three words of importance in the title of this debate, and I will try, since Mr. Bradlaugh has experienced difficulty in understanding me, whether I can tell him more distinctly what I mean by them. Those three words are "reasonable," "worship," "God." When I say it is reasonable to do a thing, I do not mean that I can demonstrate to you with the precision of mathematics that every proposition, the truth of which is assumed in that act, is true; but I do mean that the propositions, on the assumption of which the act proceeds, are, at least, sufficiently probable to win the verdict of an unbiassed judgment, and that the act itself is likely to be found to be a good. Mr. Bradlaugh himself has defined "worship" as including "prayer, praise, sacrifice, offerings, solemn services, adoration, and personal prostration." If Mr. Bradlaugh will kindly occupy his next fifteen minutes by defining to me exactly what he means by each of those terms, I may be better able to tell him whether I include them all in worship, and whether he has left anything out. But at present I do not find that any one of them is simpler or more comprehensible than the term worship, while "prayer, praise, sacrifice, and offerings," each might mean at least two very different things; "solemn services" is hopelessly vague; "adoration," as I understand it, is included in some of the others; and before we know what "personal prostration" means, we must define "person"—no easy matter—and then explain what we mean by the "prostration" of that person (laughter and applause). Meanwhile, I have described, at the very outset, that energy of my soul which I call worship, namely, that in which I address myself to God as to one immeasurably surpassing me in goodness, in wisdom, in power, in love (hear, hear). I don't think this is plainer than the good old Saxon word "worship;" I think that word conveys a pretty clear meaning to most men. But Mr. Bradlaugh finds it easier to understand long phrases than simple Saxon words; and my only fear now is that he will want me to define all the words in my definition—(laughter)—and though I am ready enough to do that, I fear it would take a week (renewed laughter, and hear, hear). God:—You ask me to define God, and you say I have not in any way done so. You quote the metaphysical definition of Flint, and want me to enter into metaphysics. What do you mean by defining? Do you mean to draw a circle round God, so as to separate him from all else? If you do, I reply, I can't; because, as far as I can see, or my imagination can extend, I discern no boundaries to God. But if you mean to ask simply what *I mean* by God, I mean—and I said this again and again last night—the source of the command that comes to me to do right, to abjure wrong; the source of the peace that comes to me even in pain, when I have done right, and of the remorse that comes to me even in prosperity when I have done ill. I mean also the source—which I believe to be identical — of the wondrous sense of a divine presence which seizes me in the midst of nature's sublimest scenes — ay, and even of nature's awful catastrophes. I mean also the source of the moral and spiritual strength that comes to me in response to the worship which my soul pours forth; and if you want to know what I mean by my soul, I mean myself. What else besides the source of these things God may be, I cannot tell you. It is only so—in his relation to me—that I directly know him. Beyond that he is the subject of philosophy, but not of immediate knowledge. I believe him to be very much more; but that does not affect the reasonableness of worshipping him, and that is the subject of our debate (hear, hear). So that I cannot define God in the way I can define Nottingham, or Europe, or the earth (hear, hear). I cannot tell how much is included in his being; how much, if any, is excluded. I can tell you what he is to me, in relation to me— and that is the only way in which any entity can be defined— and I can tell you what other men testify by word, by deed, by martyrdom, he is to them (hear, hear). Beyond that I have no instruments by which to measure; and therefore I take up no pen with which to write down the measurements, or define (applause). But Mr. Bradlaugh says if we cannot exactly define an object we are incapable of exact thought or belief concerning it. Did Mr. Bradlaugh do algebra at school? That most exact and prosaic science consists largely in reasoning about unknown quantities ; that is, about some x or y, of which you only know that it has some one or perhaps two definite relations to certain other things. You don't know what x or y is in itself—only some function by which it is related to a and b and c. From that relation you reason, and sometimes from it you get by subtle processes to infer a vast deal more, and it will perhaps prove just from that relation that x must be such and such a number, or that it must be infinite. Does Mr. Bradlaugh say we can have no exact thought about the x in the algebraic equation, before we have worked out the whole sum ? Yes, we know it in its relations or some of them. Yet the very essence of algebra is that x is undefined. The human soul is the a, b, or c, the well-known, the familiar ; God is the x, related wondrously thereto, yet none has ever yet worked out that sum. The supremest philosophers, who here are school-boys indeed, have only displayed workings on their slates which, to use again mathematical language, show that x approaches towards a limit which is equal to infinity (hear, hear). But Mr. Bradlaugh says there should be no belief in that which we cannot define. Now, I challenge Mr. Bradlaugh in all respect and sincerity to define *himself* (applause). If he declines or fails, I will not say we must cease to believe in Mr. Bradlaugh, but that is the necessary inference from his maxims. Mr. Bradlaugh says all experience must be the experience of the senses. By which sense does he experience love, indignation, or all the varied sentiments which bind him to his fellow-men and women (applause)? Mr. Bradlaugh told us in his concluding speech last night that no experience of another man's can be anything at all to him until tested by his own. Is, then, a man born blind unreasonable if he believes that others have experience of some wonderful sensation, making objects very vividly present to them, which they call sight ? Shall the man born deaf say he does not believe there is such a thing as sound ? I know not whether Mr. Bradlaugh has any personal experience of the heat of the torrid zone. Does he believe it ? Has he tested the height of Mont Blanc ? If not, does he hold his belief in suspense as to whether it is 15,000 feet high or not ? The fact is the enormous majority of the beliefs on which we act every day of our lives with perfect confidence are founded either on sheer Faith, untested and by us untestable, or on Testimony, that is the recorded experience of others which we have not tested. But Mr. Bradlaugh says that if the alleged experience of another is "abnormal" we must not believe it. He did not define "abnormal," and I want to know who is to be judge whether my experience of the command that comes to me in conscience is abnormal or not. Mr. Bradlaugh? This audience? With confidence I accept the verdict of any gathering of my fellow-men and women, knowing that my experience herein has a sure echo in their own. But Mr. Bradlaugh says, if someone said a room ran a race, you would call him a lunatic. That argument means nothing, or else it means that Martineau and Newman, and all great and good who have recognised God—ay, and Voltaire and Thomas Paine—Theists both—are to be counted lunatics (hear, hear). Time has prevented—I hope it may not still prevent—my stating clearly what I mean, when I proceed on philosophical grounds to allege my belief that there is an intelligent cause. "Intelligent" I shall not stop to define, unless I am challenged to it, because I presume intelligence in you (applause). "If there were no such supreme intelligence," says Mr. Voysey, "the universe, supposing it to be self-evolved (and of course unconscious, since it is not intelligent) has only just come into self-consciousness through one of its parts—viz., man. It had been, so to speak, asleep all these cycles of ages till man was born and his intellect dawned upon the world, and, for the first time, the universe realised its own existence through the intelligent consciousness of one of its products. I do not think absurdity could go further than that. If there be no self conscious intelligence but man, then the universe is only just now, through man, becoming aware of its own existence" (hear, hear, and applause). "Cause," Mr. Bradlaugh, I think, has defined, in language which included the words, "means towards an end." A mean or means, however, is, by the very conception of the word, the second term in a series of three of which the end is the third, and "means" implies some power making use of those means, and that power is the first term in the series. Now, I claim that cause is that first term, whether there be two more, or only one. By "cause" I mean—and you mean, if you will search your thought—the initiating power, that which begins to produce an effect. Now, my mind is so constituted that to speak to me of a power which initiates effects, yet is not conscious, intelligent, is sheer nonsense; therefore I hold the power which displays itself as one in the uniformity of the laws of nature, and lies behind all phenomena—the growth of the grass, the rush of the cataract, the breath of the air, the stately sailing of the stars through their geometric paths, to be intelligent, conscious, to do it all by distinct purpose; and I can in no way otherwise conceive. I conceive this source of the geometric motion of all the spheres and of the minutest dance of protoplasm in the nettle's sting as always, everywhere, of purpose producing these effects. And the worship which I gave God as I know him in relationship to me is refined and glorified by the conception which thus dawns on me of his being. And in the words of François Marie Arouet Voltaire, I commune thus with myself: " Where," says he, " is the eternal geometrician? Is he in one place, or in all places without occupying space? I know not. Has he arranged all things of his own substance? I know not. Is he immense without quantity and without quality? I know not. All I know is, that we must adore him and be just " (loud applause).

MR. BRADLAUGH: It is perfectly true that what I have said here I have said before, and very much of what I have said I have printed before. I am quite sure that Mr. Armstrong did not intend that as any blame upon me. [MR. ARMSTRONG: Certainly not.] In fact, if any advantage accrued, it would accrue to him, because, having what I had to say on the subject to refer to, he would be better able to answer it by previous preparation. Why I mention it is because one person seemed to think that it was very reprehensible on my part to say here anything that was not perfectly new. I make no claim to originality, but try to say the truest thing I can in the clearest way I can (hear, hear, and applause). Then I am told that I did not pay attention enough to what was said last night about the functions of the voice of God. I have been told to-night that the idea of righteousness and rectitude has always been one and the same amongst all human beings, from the savage to the highest intellect. If telling me so is evidence of it, then, of course, I must be content. But, unfortunately, I am not content, but say that the evidence is all the other way (hear, hear, and a laugh). I have read carefully Wake's latest book on the evolutions of morality, tracing out the growth of notions of morality amongst savages. I have read Tylor, Broca, Lubbock, Agassiz, Gliddon, Pritchard, Lawrence, and I think I am familiar with the best of ancient and modern authors on the subject; and I say it is absolutely contrary to the fact that the notions of morality are, and always have been identical from the lowest savage to the highest intellect. It is absolutely contrary to the fact that one and the same idea of right always and everywhere prevails (hear, hear). It is not a question of my opinion ; it is a question of the conclusive evidence laboriously collected on the subject, and I am sorry to have to put it in that plain and distinct way (hear, hear). Then I am told, and I am sure Mr. Armstrong would not have said that unless he thought he did, that he carefully separated last night the lower instincts which were not included in conscience from the higher mental qualities. But to my memory this was not so, and I have read the whole of the speeches to-day in the reporter's notes, and I must say I found nothing of the kind. Now we have a greater difficulty. How much and how many—how much of the mental instincts, and how many of the mental faculties —are we to class as going to make up conscience, and how much not ? I do not pretend to make the classification. It rests upon the person who has the burden of proof here. I deny there has been, as yet, even an attempt at classification, and I call for some statement which shall enable me to understand that ; without it is to be foregone. Then I had it returned upon me that I had no right to criticise this world unless I could conceive a better. The very act of criticism involves the conception of the better. When I point out something insufficient or wrong, that criticism implies the conception of something conceivably better if that were changed. If you want, now, an illustration of something possibly better, I would point to the famine in China. There, actually, millions of people are dying for want of food, and, for the purpose of sustaining life a little longer in themselves, the members of families are eating their own relations. If I were God I should not tolerate that—(applause)—nor could I worship a God who does. Mr. Armstrong, in his speech, pointed out what he terms an intelligent purpose. It may be for an intelligent purpose that millions of the Chinese should die of starvation, and actually eat one another for want of food ; but if it is, I cannot understand the goodness of the intelligent purposer. You cannot take one illustration and say that it is the work of an intelligent person, and then take another and say that it is not. If it is the intelligence of God displayed in one case it must be in another, unless Mr. Armstrong contends that there are a number of Gods, amongst which number there must be a good many devils (laughter and loud applause). There are many things of a similar kind I could point out, and ask the same question with regard to; where is the intelligence of God as displayed in permitting the Bulgarian atrocities, the Russo-Turkish war, the Greek insurrection—or in the world nearer home, its crime, misery, and want (hear, hear, and applause). I do not draw the same moral from the story of the starving woman that Mr. Armstrong would draw. While you thank God for the crime, pauperism, misery, and poverty, I say that you are degrading yourself. The Atheist deplores the misery, the poverty, and the crime, and does all he can to prevent it by assisting the sufferers to extricate themselves, instead of spending his time in blessing and praising a God for sending the woe and attributing it to his superior intelligence (applause). Then there was an astounding statement which came more in the sermon part of the speech than in the argumentative portion of it (laughter). Perhaps that may account for the wealth of its assumption, and also for deficiency of its basis. It was that freedom, happiness, and virtue, through the power of God, were continually winning their way. How is it that an intelligent and omnipotent God does not look after them more, and see that they overcome opposition a little faster than they have done? Mr. Armstrong says that I fight shy of experience. I don't do anything of the kind. I fight shy of experience which will not submit itself to any test; I fight shy of experience which cannot bear examination and investigation; I fight shy of such experience only. Our friend gives us the experience of a dying girl. Now, I do not mean to say that every religion in the world has not been a consolation to dying people—that belief in a God has not been a consolation to persons who have enjoyed the full power of their mental faculties on their death-beds. Since I was in America some time ago I saw a copy of a sermon preached by a New York clergyman, who had attended, what he believed to be the dying bed of an Atheist, and he said that he hoped that Christians would learn to die as bravely and as calmly as the Atheist seemed prepared to die. Luckily that Atheist did not die. He is alive tonight to answer for himself (applause and hear, hear). I don't think an illustration of personal experience in that way can go for much. The man and woman who die in possession of their faculties, with strong opinions, will generally die strong in those opinions. Men have been martyred for false gods as well as for the one you would have me worship. It is useless to make this kind of an appeal in a discussion, in which there was room and need for much else. Heavenly stars, a crown, and that kind of thing are not as certain as they ought to be in order to be treated as material in this discussion. And then Mr. Armstrong says what he would do and how he would feel if he were an Atheist. Charles Reade wrote a novel, which he entitled " Put yourself in his Place." Mr. Armstrong has been trying to put himself in the Atheist's place, but he has not been very successful (hear, hear). The Atheist does not think that all the evil which exists in this world is without remedy; he does not think that there is no possible redemption from sorrow, or that there is no salvation from misery (hear, hear). He thinks and believes that the knowledge of to-day a little, and to-morrow more, and the greater knowledge of the day that will yet come, will help to redeem, will help to rescue the inhabitants of this world from their miserable position : and further, that this is not to be in some world that is to come, but in the world of the present, in which the salvation is self-worked out (loud applause). The Atheist will not make promises of something in the future as a compensation for the present miseries of man. Instead of saying that for prayers and worship the poor woman or man will have the bread of life in future, he tries to give her and him the strength to win bread here to sustain and preserve life as long as it is possible to do so (applause). The diadems. too—which our friend has to offer to the poor—which are to be worn in heaven by those who have had no clothes here —possess no attraction to the Atheist ; therefore he does not offer them, but, instead, tries to develop such self-reliant effort as may clothe and feed those who are naked and hungry while they are here. He directs his efforts towards human happiness in the present, and believes that in the future humanity must be triumphant over misery, want, and wrong (applause). A diadem of celestial glory may or may not be a very good thing ; of that I do not look upon myself as a judge, so long as I have no belief in its possibility. That there is much misery and suffering in the world I know, and it rests with Mr. Armstrong to prove whether it is better to try and remedy it here or to worship its author in the doubtful endeavour to obtain as recompense a crown of celestial glory (hear, hear, and applause). But which

God is it that we are to worship? Is it the Mahometan God, or the Jewish God? Is it one of the Gods of the Hindus? Is it the Christian's God? If so, which sect of Christians? You must not use phrases which mean different things in different mouths (hear, hear). Then we come to definitions, and, having objected that there was no necessity for defining, or having objected that defining would not make things more clear, with the skill and tact of a practical debater, my friend goes through every word (laughter). Prayer, we were told, has two distinct meanings. Might I ask in which sense it was used in the first speech made last night? You did not tell us then that prayer had two senses. I ask why you did not tell us? I might have thought it was one fashion when you meant another. I ask what meaning you meant when you used it? What two senses has prayer towards God?—in which of the two senses did you use prayer—and, knowing it had two meanings, why did you not tell us in which sense you used it? Then praise, too, you said, is to thank God for his goodness; and as you used the word many times last night you knew what you meant by it, having relied upon it so firmly that it seemed to be an evidence of God's existence (applause). By sacrifice I mean an act of real cowardice. The coward does not dare to pay in his own person for the wrong which he has done, so he offers something or somebody weaker in his stead. He tries by offering a sacrifice to avert the vengeance which would fall—and, according to his creed, ought to fall—upon himself. Sacrifice is the act of a coward (applause). Offerings are of flowers, of fruits; offerings of young animals, lambs, kids; sometimes the offerings are things which come the nearest to their hands; sometimes the sacrifice consists of inanimate things which had a special value to the worshipper; sometimes the first fruits of their fields or flocks, which they offer to the source, as they think, of the plenty in those fields and flocks. In later times, offerings have got to be much more complex; but even now you will still find them, in modified fashions, in the Churches of England and Rome. The mutual system is that which operates in every form of worship which makes any sort of claim to religion. The word "worship" was only used as a general word which covers the whole of those forms, leaving our friends to select and repudiate, and in any case the burden is on Mr. Armstrong to make the meaning clear (hear,

hear). I read the whole of the speeches of last night without finding any repudiation or question about the definitions I presented ; and I submit it is scarcely fair, after what has passed, to ask me to further define them at this late stage of the debate. I should have had no objection had it been invited at the earliest outset (applause). Well, now, we have worship defined as "the energy of my soul." Well, but you have not explained your soul. Why do you call it soul ? Where is its place in your body ? Is there anything about soul you can notice so as to enable me to know anything at all about it ? Will you take your definition of soul from Voltaire, whom you have quoted against me ? When you reply, will you tell us what Voltaire, Professor Newman, Paine, or Martineau say upon the subject of God, and in which of their writings you will find that which all the others would accept as a definition ? You must remember the Theist of Paine's time is not the Theist of to-day, and I want you to tell us what are the specific opinions of each of those you have quoted—of Francis William Newman, of John William Newman, of Martineau, of Thomas Paine, of Voltaire—as to the questions I have asked (applause). Which of the Gods is it that I am to understand Mr. Armstrong as defending and asking me to worship (loud applause) ?

MR. ARMSTRONG : Mr. Chairman, Ladies, and Gentlemen,—I am somewhat at a loss as to which of the numerous questions I am to answer first. I shall not take them in any logical order, but simply pick out of my note-book the most important of them. Mr. Bradlaugh has said that the act of criticism of the world implied the conception of a better world. Mr. Bradlaugh has tried to describe his conception of the better world, and I have tried in my previous speeches to show that he would not make it better. And I again submit that, instead of being better, it would be worse (hear, hear). He says he does not draw the same conclusion from that poor woman in the cellar that I do. He says that while you are content to suffer, you degrade yourself. Now, there are two kinds of content. You may be content like the sloth or the sluggard, or you may be content like that poor woman, who while trying to improve her position, still remained poor to the end of her days, and yet at the same time felt the peace of God in her heart. Does the belief in a God, as a fact, make men less energetic and vigorous in improving their own condition, or trying to improve that of others? I don't believe it does (applause). I believe you have Theists as well as Atheists, who devote their kindly sympathies to the good of their fellow creatures. They are content in one sense and discontent in another sense. They have that holy discontent which makes them anxious to remedy the world's evil, and that content which makes them see God, who is working from evil to good (applause). We have been told by Mr. Bradlaugh what the Atheist will do; how he will give the bread of this life to the hungry child; the Theist will do the same (applause). The Theist will—but no, I will not institute these comparisons; we are each, I feel sure, striving to do our best; so I won't enter into comparisons (rounds of applause). He says it is unreasonable to worship an insoluble proposition. A proposition is a grammatical term signifying a statement, and I am not aware that I asked anyone to worship a statement or proposition at all. I have called upon you to worship God (applause). He says I did not separate the lower instincts from the higher mental qualities in man. I do not say I did. But I did separate the lower instincts from the voice of God in conscience. I said that it was entirely distinct from the lower instincts in man. I said that the voice had a right to command and rule these lower instincts (hear, hear). He asks me which God it is that I am preaching. I will tell you what God I ask you to worship—the best that you can conceive, whatsoever it is (applause). I want you all to worship the best that you can conceive (rounds of applause). If the Hindu's idea is the best he can conceive, let him, by all means, worship it (hear, hear). If the Jew's God is the best he can imagine, let him pay homage to it. If the Christian's idea of God is the highest he can conceive, let him be true to it and worship it, and it will make him a nobler man (applause). It is not mere names which signify in a matter of this kind. Though each sect may give him different names, it is still the same God (hear, hear). Mr. Bradlaugh wants to know which of them all I uphold as God; which of the different types I acknowledge, or ask you to acknowledge. Is it the God of Martineau, of Newman, of Parker, or of whom else? I say it is that which is common among them all—namely, the conception of goodness and excellence which you will find in every one of their definitions. It is that God which they

all recognise, and concerning which they only go wrong
when they begin to try and define it metaphysically
(hear, hear). Mr. Bradlaugh wants me to define God;
further than I have done so, I cannot. In the words of
the Athanasian Creed an attempt is made to define the un-
definable. The Athanasian Creed tries to explain the whole
of that which overrules the universe instead of describing
simply that which is in relationship to you. I have always
been under the supposition that that was a practice of the
theologian which had greatly retarded the progress of the
world. Mr. Bradlaugh spoke of prayer as implying a hope
—a hope to induce God to do what he would not do without prayer; and he wanted to know in what sense I used
the word "prayer" in my speeches. I have not used the
word "prayer" without describing what I meant. At least,
I have not done so to my knowledge; if I have, I am
sorry for it (applause). Mr. Bradlaugh says that prayer implies a hope of inducing God to do what he would not do
without it. For my part, I doubt whether some things
that have been called prayers, such as the prayers for the
recovery of the Prince of Wales—(loud hisses and laughter)
—for wet weather, and for fine weather, have very much
influenced the divine counsels (hear, hear and applause).
But what do I mean by prayer? As I have said before,
the addressing of my soul to this power which I feel and
recognise above me; and the law of the answer of prayer—
and it is as much a law as any law of nature—is that they
who do thus energise themselves towards God become thereby
more susceptible to the energising of God towards them. The
law is that he who energises or addresses himself towards
God, consciously, reverently, and of set purpose, thereby sets
at motion a law by which he becomes more susceptible to
God's addressing of himself to him, and so he gains to himself the strength, moral and spiritual, which we find in prayer
(hear, hear). Mr. Bradlaugh picked out one of the words from
his own definition of worship. By sacrifice he said he meant
the act of a man who was too cowardly to bear the result of his
own actions. As far as that definition goes, I may say I do
not include it in my idea of worship (applause). Now, sir,
I have striven to the best of my power to be precise and
clear in my words. It is true I have not dealt with the
matter from a platform purely metaphysical. I am a positivist
in most things, understanding by a positivist one who founds
his philosophy on observed phenomena. I have passed out

of the stage in which men believe that theological theories will solve all the problems of the universe. I have passed out of the stage in which Mr. Bradlaugh now is, in which metaphysics are looked upon as the best ground of reasoning we can have. I have passed into the stage in which positive thought, the recognition of phenomena, is recognised as the best starting-point we can have from which to get at the truth. Auguste Comte traces the progress of the thought of the world and of the individual from the theological stage to the metaphysical stage, and from that to the positive stage. I invite Mr. Bradlaugh to look at things from that stage, and to see whether he cannot make his thoughts clearer by the use of the positive method than by the use of the metaphysical (loud applause).

MR. BRADLAUGH: The curious thing is that I have never used the word metaphysics, and I have offered to affirm no proposition that does not relate to phenomena. I am astounded to hear that I am a metaphysician (laughter and applause). Is it because I only used language which I can make clear that my opponent gave me that title? It is because he does not use language that is related to phenomena that he is obliged to commend his Theism by speaking of it as a problem which is insoluble (applause). I have not done anything, as far as my case is concerned, except use language relating to phenomena. Now, I have only a few moments, and this speech will be my last in this debate. I would, therefore, like you to see the position in which we stand. I am told that the improvement I would suggest would in no sense tend to virtue. I must refer again to the state of things in China, where the members of the same family are eating each other for want of food. Would it not tend to virtue if their condition was remedied (applause)? I wish my friend and myself to look at things from this point of view, and, as he is in the positive way of thinking, let him put himself in the same state as they are, and then ask whether an amendment of the condition would not tend to greater virtue (renewed applause). What God is it that we are to worship? Oh, the God it is reasonable to worship is the best we can conceive—but no conception has yet been put before us. You have been told a great deal about stars, but the more important facts and arguments still remain unchallenged (hear, hear). Now, I am asked, does belief in God hinder philanthropy? Yes, when it is held as those do hold it in some parts of the world, who think that God has designed, in his thought and intelligence, and for good purposes, that a famine should take place, such as the one in China (hear, hear). There are at least people among the Mahometans and the Hindus whose virtue has been clearly shown to have suffered much more from religion than from civilisation (applause). The case put as to prayer is one which I think has something peculiar about it. We are told first of the law of prayer, which is said to be as much a law of nature as any other law. Well, now, by law of nature (MR. ARMSTRONG: Hear, hear)—I don't know if I am misrepresenting you—I only mean observed order of happening (pouring water from glass); I do not mean that there has been some direction given that this water shall fall, but that, given the conditions, the event ensues. Law of nature is order of sequence or concurrence, the observed order of phenomena. What observed order of phenomena is there in the order of prayer? When the prayer prays "himself he sets a law in motion." Is this so? We are told that the prayer for the recovery of the Prince of Wales did not much tend to alter the divine counsel. Mr. Armstrong did not tell you how he knew that. His own admission here proves that prayer is sometimes offered in vain, taking the observed order of its phenomena (hear, hear). He spoke of the holy discontent in pious men which set them to seek to remedy evil. Holy discontent against the state of things which God in his intelligent purpose has caused! Then the holy discontent is dissatisfaction with God's doings. How can you worship the God with whom you are dissatisfied (applause)? But what is the truth of the matter? In the early ages of the world man saw the river angry and prayed to the river-god; but science has dispelled the river-god, and has substituted for prayer, weirs, locks, dykes, levels, and flood-gates (hear, hear). You see the same thing over the face of nature wherever you go. What you have found is this: that in the early ages of the world gods were frightful, gods were monstrous, gods were numerous, because ignorance predominated in the minds of men. The things they came in contact with were not understood, and no investigation then took place; men worshipped. But gradually men learned first dimly, then more clearly, and god after god has been demolished as science has grown. The best attempt at conception of God is always the last conception of him, and this because God has to give way to science. The best conception of God is in substituting humanity for deity, the getting rid of, and turning away from, the whole of those conceptions and fancies which men called God in the past, and which they have ceased to call God now (applause). Mr. Armstrong thought that it was because men had given different names to God that I tried to embarrass him by bidding him choose between them. It was not so; it is the different characteristics and not the different names that I pointed out as a difficulty. We have gods of peace, gods of war, gods of love, a god of this people, or of that tribe, a god of the Christians, a god of misery, of terror, of beneficence—these are all different suppositions held by men of the gods they have created. It has well been said that the gods have not created the men, but the men have created the gods, and you can see the marks of human handicraft in each divine lineament (applause). I cannot hope, pleading here to-night, to make many converts. I can and do hope that all of you will believe that the subject treated wants examination far beyond the limits of this short debate. I have a very good hope indeed, and really believe that some good has been done when it can be shown that two men of strong opinions, and earnest in their expressions, can come together without one disrespectful word to each other, or want of respect in any way; without any want of due courtesy to the other; and with a great desire to separate the truth and the falsehood (applause). If there has been unwittingly anything disrespectful on my part, I am sorry for it. I have to thank Mr. Armstrong for coming forward in the manner in which he has done, and I can only ask all to use their services in making the spread of virtue, truth, and justice easier than it has been. I am aware that I have nominally a vast majority against me, but I do not fear on that ground, and still shall continue to point out falsehood wherever I may find it. At any rate, the right of speech is all I ask, and that you have conceded. I have only an earnest endeavour to find out as much as I can that will be useful to my fellows, and to tell them as truly as I can how much I grasp. It is for you—with the great harvest of the unreaped before you—who can do more than I, to gather and show what you have gathered; it is for you who have more truth to tell it more efficiently; and when you answer me I put it to you that so far as the world has redeemed itself at all, it has only redeemed itself by shaking off in turn the Theistic religions which have grown and decayed. So far, it seems to be a real and solid redemption (applause). When religion was supreme through the ignorance of men, the people were low down indeed, and a few devoted men had to grapple with the hereafter theory and all the content with present wrong which the belief in it maintained. Take a few hundred years ago, when there was little or no scepticism in the world. Only a very few able to be heretical—the mass unable and too weak to doubt or endure doubt. Look at the state of things then, and look at it now. Could a discussion like this have taken place then? No. But it can since the printing-press has helped us; it can since the right of speech has been in good part won. Two hundred years ago it could not have been. Two hundred years ago I could not have got the mass of people together to listen as you have listened last night and to-night, and had not men treated your religion as I treat it, we should not have the right of meeting even now (applause). If you want to convince men like myself, hear us; answer us if you can—say what you have to say without making it more bitter than we can bear. We must believe it if it is reasonable, and if not we must reject it. So long as there is any wrong to redeem we shall try to redeem it ourselves (applause). We may be wrong in this, but at least we do our part. I do not mean that in the same ranks as my friend there are not men as sincere and as earnest, men as devoted, men as human-redemption seeking as myself, but I, or the best of those for whom I plead, urge that their humanity is not the outcome of their theology (applause). Then their experience of right, their hope of life, and their experience of truth rest entirely on what they do here. And I will ask you this: do you not think it is quite possible, as Lessing says, that he who thinks he grasps the whole truth may not even grasp it at all? like the one deceived by the juggler's trick, he may think he holds something in his hand, but when it is opened it is empty (hear, hear). Take the truth as you can—not from me, not from him, not from any one man. There is none of the bad which is all bad, none of the good all good, none of the truth all true: it is for you to select, to weigh, to test for yourselves (hear, hear). Many of us stumble in trying to carry the torch in dark places in the search for truth, but even in our trembling steps the sparks we scatter may enable some to find the grains of truth we miss ourselves (loud and prolonged applause).

Mr. Armstrong: Mr. Bradlaugh, the body to which I belong also have the majority against them; over that we can shake hands. Let us try, each in our own way, as may best seem to us, to serve what we hold to be true (applause). Depend upon it, whether there be a God or not, we each shall do best so. If there be no God, then you tell me I shall still do well to serve humanity. And if there be a God, he will gather you also, my brother, to his arms, so long as you are true—true and absolutely sincere in those convictions which come to you from the reason which he has given you (loud applause). You have told us that while religion held sway men were down-trodden. While superstition held sway it is true they were (applause); while false ideas of a cruel and lustful God held sway, it is true they were (applause); but just in proportion as men's thoughts of God have purified and clarified, just in proportion as they have restored to Christianity its sweet meaning, just in that proportion religion has risen to be a power in the world of all that is good and sweet and holy (applause). Now, sir, to speak of what I said about the prayers for the recovery of the Prince of Wales. I said I thought they had been of little avail. But the prayer for spiritual purity from a Christian man does win its answer by a law—a law of nature, I will now say, since you have defined a law of nature as the observed sequence of phenomena; but I dared not so call it until I knew what your definition of nature might be. But let us come back from these philosophisings, in which it is so easy to go wrong, to the test of experience. Mr. Bradlaugh says I do not submit the experiences of which I have spoken, to the test. I invite you to test them, and see whether Mr. Bradlaugh has upset them or not. If you test them fairly and then find them false, then come and tell me so. They are neither uncommon nor abnormal experiences, but the experiences of nearly every man and woman. It may be that their hearing is dull, but still they know the voice. You all know those in which the initiative comes from God, the voice of conscience, of which I spoke; you all know the solemn feeling which comes over you in the presence of the majesty of nature. You all may know the other things in which you have to take the initiative. Heed those things whether you believe they come from God or not, and you all may know the other—that of worship —and its answer. My contention solely is, that it would be reasonable for you to seek for that experience, that it is reasonable in us to practise it (hear, hear). And now I will tell you a little story for the end of this debate, of a little family of children; and as I shall not found any argument upon it, I do not think it will be unfair. They sat one Christmas Eve in a chamber where the wintry gloom of early twilight fell. The eldest son sat and talked of the goodness of their father, and how, from the earliest days he could recollect, his tenderness had sheltered him, and how he seemed to have a heart to love every little child all through the world, and how he was surely even now preparing some sweet surprise for them every one But John, the second boy, had lived all his life at a school on the far sea coast, where he had been sent, that rough ocean breezes might strengthen his weakly frame, and now, tanned and burly, he had just come home for Christmas, and he had not even seen his father yet. And he said he did not believe they had a father; that Theophilus, declaring he had seen him, was nothing to him, for if there was one thing he had learned at school, it was not to trust the experience of other people till tested by his own. But Edward said he, too, knew they had a father; he, too, had seen him, but he was very stern, and he thought they could all do as well without him, and what could be more unkind than to leave them there in twilight solitude on Christmas Eve. And little Tom sat apart in the very darkest corner of the room, with a tear-stained face, crying as if his heart would break, over the hard sums set him there to do, and thinking that his brothers were a selfish lot of fellows, to talk and talk, and not care for him and his hard task. And Theophilus had just come to steal his arm around little Tom's waist, and dry his tears, and try if he could not help him to do his sum, when the door of the next room was thrown open and a blaze of light flashed upon their faces, and one after the other they all rushed in and beheld their father standing by such a glorious Christmas-tree as boys never beheld before. And for each and all there were gifts so rare and precious—the very things they had longed for all the by-gone half. And for John, who had been so far away and had not known his father, there was a grasp of the father's hand so strong and tender, and a kiss from the father's lips so sweet and loving, that he felt as if he had known that dear father all his life; and as for little Tom, all his tears were dissolved in rippling laughter, and he quite forgot his sum, for on his brow was set the brightest coronet on all the tree, and they told him he should be king through all the long Christmas-day to follow. And now, dear friends, may the peace of

God which passeth all understanding, that peace which the perishing things of the world can neither give nor take away, that peace promised to the weary by our dear brother, Jesus Christ, even in the midst of all his suffering and woe, be with you for ever. Amen (applause).

MR. ARMSTRONG having sat down, rose again and said,—And now, Mr. Chairman, I desire to move to you the hearty thanks of this meeting for your conduct in the chair, for your impartial manner of ruling over us, and the kind words you have spoken. I thank you, Mr. Bradlaugh, for the courtesy and fairness with which you have conducted your part in this debate; and I thank you, sir, for presiding over us (applause).

MR. BRADLAUGH: I second that motion. I cannot say that we can thank you for your fairness, for, fortunately, you have had no opportunity of showing it. But I thank you most heartily for accepting a position which might have been one of great difficulty and the taking of which may cause you to be misrepresented. I also thank Mr. Armstrong for having met me, and for the kindly manner in which he has spoken (applause).

The vote of thanks was put and carried unanimously.

The CHAIRMAN: Ladies and Gentlemen,—the thanks which have been given to me are due rather to the gentlemen who have spoken. I cannot but praise the admirable way in which they have rendered my position almost a sinecure. This debate has shown that a subject of such great importance can be discussed fairly, liberally, honestly, as this has been, and that no danger threatens him who occupies the chair, or those who lay their honest and earnest views before you. I feel that I have derived much knowledge from the truth which has been laid before us; and I do feel that there is a growing interest in things of this sort, which is itself a proof that discussions of this kind are very useful (applause).

www.ingramcontent.com/pod-product-compliance
Lightning Source LLC
Chambersburg PA
CBHW022152090426
42742CB00010B/1477